To Charlie, always a good listener

© Nabil Shabka 2020

Contents

The Facts Are Always Changing, Like It Or Not — 1
   The Automobile Revolution — 3
   The End of the Automobile Revolution — 5

Backstory - Our History — 7
   The crawling years — 7
   The walking years — 7
   And Then Came Industrialisation — 9
   Mass Consumerism — 12
   Immigration — 16
   Globalisation — 19
   AI (Artificial Intelligence) — 22
   The Environment — 26
   Politics and Politicians — 31
   The Generational Split — 34

Wealth Inequality — 44

The Money Tree – How Things Work — 52
   Money — 52
   Crypto currencies — 56
   Interest — 59
   Banking — 66
   Retail Banking — 66
   Investment Banking — 67
   The Workers — 81

How We Got Into This Mess — 87
   Neoliberalism — 87
   Financial Deregulation — 88

How Do We Fix This Sh*t? — 95

Step One - Show Me The Money — 97
   Finance Regulation — 97
   Financial Inequality — 98
   Austerity or Trickle-Up? — 100
   Tax – The New Social — 103

Star Trek Or Blade Runner — 120
   Universal Income (UI) — 121
   Universal Healthcare (UH) — 125
   Universal Education (UE) — 127
   The Green Revolution — 129
   The People Revolution — 132

Step Two – Social Valyou — 143

Conclusion — 150

When the facts change, I change my mind.

What do you do?

John Maynard Keynes

The Facts Are Always Changing, Like It Or Not

Humankind has arrived at a very important junction in its evolution, but it doesn't even seem to realise it. There are fundamental changes occurring around us which will shape our future and we need to take them into account as we make some critical decisions, yet it's business as usual. We're trying to solve today's problems, using yesterday's tools, but not thinking about tomorrow and where we're going. We need to address this, and we can begin by asking, what's the big picture?

What is important to us? What do we value? What kind of life do we want?

We seem to be careening through this period of massive change with no destination in mind. Sometimes, the best way forward is to take a step back and start from the beginning. Now is such a time. Let's imagine future generations. In an ideal world, what will motivate people? What will their purpose be? Why will they get up in the morning? And, as its designers, how would we like it to look? Armed with this, our choices will be clearer, and we can plan a route forward.

Once we have an idea of this big picture, we need to imagine our future with those things in place and work out what we can do to our existing infrastructure to support this. We need to think about what we have done right and what we have not done so well. We can then work backwards and explore the choices we need to make to stand a better chance of realising our goals. After all, we can't come up with solutions if we don't first know what our objectives are.

It's exciting, and it's scary.

On the one hand, we're living longer, healthier lives than ever before and if we don't dig too deep, things actually appear quite good for many of us. We have far more consumer choices than ever before and our quality of life is high compared to previous generations. Two hundred years ago passenger trains first hit the tracks. One hundred years ago automobiles hit the road. Seventy years ago airplanes took to the air. Fifty years ago we landed on the moon. Twenty years ago the first passengers entered space. Now we have driverless cars.

Imagine what we could be doing in another hundred years.

Imagine what we won't be doing!

At the same time though, there are some pretty hairy and intertwined issues facing society that we urgently need to deal with. For example, there's the end of the automobile revolution and its associated job losses. AI (Artificial Intelligence) and ML (Machine Learning) are everywhere and untamed, doing good and doing bad, changing the way we work, whilst spiralling debt and rising financial inequality are changing the way we live. The environment we so easily plundered now desperately needs our help. Social care and healthcare, that have benefited our lives, are now straining under huge new demands, since we're living longer than ever before and expect more from our services.

And, very crucially, what is our purpose? What is our value?

Throughout human history our purpose has been pretty straight forward – survival: through production of food, shelter, clothing, and then, luckily for us, health, education and social services. On a global scale, you may be surprised to hear that we've almost accomplished this. Hans and Ola Rosling's *Factfulness* (2018) provides pleasantly surprising statistics on this subject.[1] Once production for survival ceases to be our prime objective and value creator, what happens next? It's a puzzle.

It's far harder to do a jigsaw puzzle without having an overall picture to keep referring back to. Since people and society have changed so much in the past one hundred years, we need to create a new picture to guide us. So, it's time to make some very important choices about where we want to be. We need to decide which direction to point ourselves and we need to think about what kind of society we want to live in.

As there are so many interwoven issues, trying to understand each piece in detail is far too great a task for just one book, so let's work with generalisations in order not to lose focus and get bogged down. Sure, there are exceptions to almost everything, but if we focus too closely on the detail of those 'trees', we'll lose sight of the bigger picture of the 'forest'.

Looking at the forest, we can agree that most of us want the same basic thing: a comfortable, safe and healthy environment that we can share with family and friends. In other words, around the world, people would like a healthy earth (the environment) populated with healthy people (mentally and physically). That's a good place to start. Let's build from there.

We need to imagine people's lives in the future. What will they be doing to enable this healthy world that they will inhabit? What will make them feel socially valuable? While so much has changed so quickly already, there's a lot more to come. These next steps won't be incremental though. They'll be evolutionary.

We're evolving into uncharted territory and 'there be dragons' as well as huge opportunities.

The smart recognise change coming and adjust accordingly as best they can - if they can.

Let's be smart.

The Automobile Revolution

One of the biggest changes facing us is the end of the automobile revolution. Where we are today is in many ways due to the car. The automobile was the job creator of the past. That is about to be over. The social impact will be massive.

The automobile revolution kicked off after the Second World War. It was the foundation of seventy years of global growth and is what created and facilitated our modern consumer society. Automobile production linked (and still links) many different jobs to create, produce, market and support them. A car may be assembled in a factory, but its parts come from countless sub suppliers scattered around the world. Whether it is steel, minerals, plastic, rubber, design sales and marketing or assembly, testing and racing, lots of people are involved.

We are where we are because of it. The automobile revolution gave us freedom and created jobs. Not just the ones related to manufacturing and other obvious ones, such as truck driver, taxi driver, bus driver and delivery driver, but also a huge host of others. These include non-obvious ones as well, at least until you think about it, such as advertising and parking.

There's servicing, repairs, insurance, marketing, design, automation, fuel, oil, washing, road creation, rentals, financing, motels, driver's education, diners, parking, speeding tickets, plus all those TV and print ads. Someone was paid to create them, while others were paid to display them. And the list goes on.

The first thing that people in developing countries do when they start to have money is to buy a car and then that car stimulates all the other related industries.

There were 94 million cars manufactured globally in 2016 and if automobiles were their own country it would be the 6th biggest economy in the world. [2] And that's without all the other related jobs.

In the US, there are still 1,605,000 jobs producing cars and 213,000 in the UK. A further three times that are indirectly related to the production (dealers and suppliers). That's a total of over 6 million production related jobs in the US and over 800,000 in the UK.[3] In the EU, it's 13.8 million people accounting for 6.1% of all jobs.[4] That's just the manufacturing and distribution bit.

In the US, since 1996 the most common employment in twenty-nine of the fifty states is trucking.5 There are 3.5mn truckers and another 5.2mn related roles. One in every fifteen people in the US is connected to the trucking industry.6 It's a $700 billion gig and that doesn't include all the related services and the 7.2 million people who support it and derive a living from it.

The most common job in every state, 2014

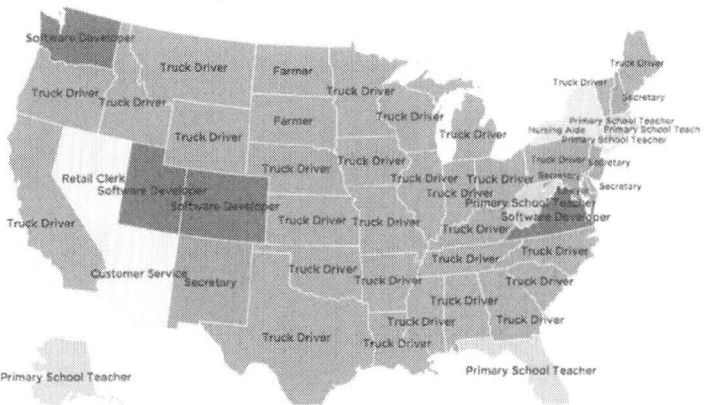

In the US, there are over 180,000 taxi drivers, 160,000 Uber drivers, 500,000 school bus drivers, and 160,000 transit bus drivers.[7]

Professional drivers account for over 2% of US employment, and then there's another 3% in supporting roles. Automobiles are a huge job generator.

As we can clearly see, the automobile revolution was central to the jobs' creation and prosperity of the late 20th century – and still is. We are here because of cars – and tractors, ships, motorcycles, and all the rest.

This type of luxury production helped create mass consumerism, which in turn, fuelled more production. These two feed off each other. Supply creates demand and demand creates supply. The previous seventy years was the age of the Automobile Revolution. What's next? How do we evolve?

The End of the Automobile Revolution

The days of our economies being driven by the automobile are about to end. Twenty years from now the landscape will be completely different. The reasons are simple – automation, ML (Machine Learning) and AI (Artificial Intelligence). The need for people in the manufacturing process and its associated roles is declining by the day.

First, vehicle manufacturing is becoming increasingly automated; the number of people required to produce more vehicles is continually decreasing. The machines are taking over production.

Second, self-driving will become the norm in the not too distant future. Not just will all those truckers', taxi drivers', bus drivers' and delivery drivers' jobs disappear, but so will all the jobs related to them – motels, servicing, petrol stations etc. In 2016 a convoy of three semi-automated trucks drove 2,000 miles from Sweden to Rotterdam.[8] The need for drivers of any variety will soon disappear.

Third, demand. Most people will stop owning cars. They'll rent them. And cars won't be cars, as we know them now, they'll be *autopods*. Some will have chairs, some beds; others will have meeting tables or coffee makers. You'll rent a small *autopod* for short journeys, a meeting *autopod* with a table for meetings, a sleeping autopod for long journeys, a big autopod for parties. It's already happening with many car-sharing companies popping up. And many young people are not even bothering to get driving licences. A driving licence used to be a rite of passage. You were an adult and had freedom when you passed your test. Now, many young people view it as an unnecessary cost and hassle.

In Japan, car-sharing company Orix noticed a strange phenomenon: 15% of the cars being rented via their app weren't being driven anywhere. Turns out that people were renting them to take naps, charge tech devices, listen to music, have lunch, watch films, store bags or have quiet conversations.[9] That's not what cars used to be used for.

The car as we know it is on the cusp of change and the automobile revolution, as the job creator of the 20th century, is about to be over. Not only will jobs and taxes disappear, but also parking fines alone are worth billions to the US and the UK. New York made $545 million in parking fines in 2016 and even Columbus Ohio made $5.2 million.[10] In England, in 2018/19, local councils made a profit of £930 million in parking fees and received a total of £1.746bn from their parking operations between 2018-19. This included £454m from penalties, which is up 6% year-on-year.[11] In London alone that was an average of £1 million a day in fees.[12]

Currently cars spend 95% of their time parked.[13] We'll have fewer of them. They'll be on the move and when they're parked, they'll be on private property. That's just the tip of the iceberg.

Think of all the knock-on effects. Jobs lost to automation in factories and services. What's going to replace this taxable income and how are all the people previously employed in automobile related industries, factories, warehouses and service jobs, going to make ends meet? How are they going to contribute to the economy?

What are we to do?

I've gotten ahead of myself and jumped the gun. Let's go back to the beginning. Let's see how we got to where we are today.

Backstory - Our History

The crawling years

Throughout humankind's history our primary motivation has been based around survival. Providing food, shelter and clothing. We were hunter-gatherers for the better part of 200,000 years. We roamed, took care of today's needs and didn't plan much for tomorrow. We may have known the good hunting and foraging grounds and even formed small units for protection and efficiency to enhance our survivability, but our needs were simple – provide a roof over our heads and put food on the table.

The walking years

We had the agricultural revolution 8,000 years ago. People found that if they stopped wandering and worked together, they could grow things on a recurring basis, they could 'farm' animals and the land, have a more reliable food supply, and they could better protect themselves. They could also plan for tomorrow. Every day need not be about survival alone. It could be about the quality of that survival. With regularity of food, shelter and clothing we could plan ahead and prepare.

As agriculture became more efficient, trade grew, and markets developed. You swapped what you over produced for what someone else over produced. Central areas, market towns, began to grow as a place to swap your wares. Efficiency in production was rewarded.

Towns formed alliances to protect themselves, and dictators - or Gods - reigned over them. They traded with other groups and due to a very hospitable natural environment, two major civilisations appeared, Egypt and China, plus several others of course. Both civilisations had a core landmass, with fresh-water river deltas and climates well suited for agriculture; land they managed and protected for thousands of years. Egypt and China were numerous in population for the time (Egypt 3 million and China 30 million) and were generally more concerned with defence and offence for defensive reasons, rather than just expanding their empires for vanity's sake. They expanded to trade, and to protect that trade. This resulted in a few thousand years of almost semi-calm.

It is no accident then that this also marked the true beginning of intellectual development for humankind. It was the first-time humanity had a chance to think, to imagine, to wonder and to dream. People had free time. The Ancient Egyptian and Chinese Civilisations created an environment that fostered the arts, maths, writing, city planning and government by making secure places for themselves. People were safe in their confines to explore, to enhance and to create new things. They began to envision and innovate and to create new products and services that increased the quality of life – new technology that made farming or defence safer and more efficient, and offered more hygiene and medical care. This is what we call civilisation. People grouped together, working for a common cause, safety, and the protection and enhancement of daily living.

This is what political groups promise, and always have promised; better ways of all this working together.

The more efficiently a person produced, the more excess they had to trade, and thus the more reward they received. This gave them something to trade for other items. The farmer exchanged with the hunter, the blacksmith and the tailor. In a family unit everyone had roles involved in producing things, supporting that process and making it as efficient as possible. Excess production could then be exchanged for other needs, and so professions developed.

Early on, we learned that pooling resources, rather than remaining independent, improved productivity and security. We specialised more and created better goods and excess production to trade. Production is what we valued. This evolved from families, tribes, villages, cities and countries to our current attempts at global. A by-product of this efficiency is that people became specialists and, as their basic needs were met easily, the focus then turned to improving the quality of those goods and services. And more 'free time' appeared.

Free time was defined as having your basic needs met and the luxury to have time that need not be utilised, 'producing' something. It was/is *your* time to do something of interest to you, that need not be productive in the traditional sense, but could be, such as tinkering and improving your production methods (because it's your passion) or doing something that eventually leads to something 'productive'. Those that enhanced this

8

process often benefitted by producing more 'over-supply', or someone else benefitted on their behalf.

Historically, while many people were making 'technological progress' on their tools and production methods, it is no accident that most of the people of note who advanced the arts, mathematics, medicine, science, exploration and astronomy were either wealthy or had wealthy patrons. They were the lucky few afforded the luxury of time to pursue their interests as their basic needs were being met.

These people's first objective was often not producing something, but exploration. Many of these pursuits nevertheless created enormous production value and got us to where we are today. But these people did not produce immediately, so they needed a patron in order to have the free time to follow their passions. Eventually, production and day-to-day improvements to products and services resulted from the implementation of this new knowledge, which in turn created further knowledge and wealth from producing and selling more.

And Then Came Industrialisation

Industrialisation increased variety and the pace of product delivery. We could produce more and faster, and a whole ecosystem was built around it. People worked in factories, were paid regular wages, and spent their money. The more that was produced, the less production cost, due to efficiencies of scale. We became experts in efficiency improvements, and in turn we could then buy more with our money. Initially, life was pretty bad for most of us, but it changed when we went from the dirty industrial revolution to the clean one – the one with health and safety creeping in – the automobile revolution.

Those closest to the top of the production spout benefitted the most, the factory/business owners, shareholders, and then staff. Our collective purpose was to make and sell stuff. The more stuff sold, the better; the wider the choice, the better to sell more and improve the quality of life. People wanted goods and services and we excelled at providing new things that we didn't even know we wanted – things that took us far beyond our basic needs and into the lifestyle zone we currently find ourselves in, a zone in which we buy things for ourselves; those things that make us live and feel better while doing so.

People had purpose working in these industries. We helped produce things, things we often bought ourselves. We earned our daily crust. We had a reason to get up in the morning. We were involved in the 'making' process and were rewarded for it. We provided a better life for our families and ourselves. We had purpose. We added value. We had value.

It was a mini golden age.

I was fortunate to grow up in this age. I have seen, am seeing, the world go from one place to another in the space of fifty years. The world is so different in 2020 than it was in 1970. The rate of change in the quality and range of our goods and services is staggering and far, far more than the previous 10,000 years combined. Wow. Aren't we lucky? Yes we are.

Using Gapminder's four income levels, most of humanity's time was spent at Level 1 and creeping into Level 2.[14]

	Level 1	Level 2
No. of people	1 billion	3 billion
Daily wage	$2	$8
Living Standard	Extreme Poverty	Poor
Water	Walk hours to get water	Half an hour to get
Food	Scramble for food, grow it	Poultry and eggs
Transport	Walking	Bicycle
Education	None	Primary school for kids
Energy	Gather firewood	Some electricity & gas
Health	Can't treat basic illnesses	Can treat minor illnesses, but can take all savings
Clothing	No shoes	Sandals
Sleeping	Mud floor	Mattress
Job	None	unskilled local work
Holidays	None	None

	Level 3	Level 4
No. of people	2 billion	1 billion
Daily wage	$32	over $32
Living Standard	Striving	Comfort
Water	Running cold water	Hot and cold
Food	Meat and variety	Varied diet
Transport	Motorcycle	Car
Education	High school for kids	University
Energy	On tap and have a fridge	On tap
Health	Can treat minor illnesses, have some savings to fall back on	Healthcare available
Clothing	Shoes	Wardrobe
Sleeping	Kids shared bedrooms	Kids have own rooms
Job	Factory /multiple jobs	Good job
Holidays	1 day to the beach	1 week +

From hunter-gatherers, to farming, to industrialisation and mass farming, humankind has been involved in a never-ending quest to produce more, and better. More production, as long as consumption demand was there, resulted in more value (money) to the producer and our quality of life improved. We excelled at the production of goods and services to the point that in most of the world we are now focused on quality, not quantity. Levels 3 and 4 people now account for over 40% of the world's population.

Globally, 91% of children are vaccinated, 90% of children have at least nine years of schooling, 50% have a smart mobile phone and the list goes on.[15] Things are actually pretty good.

I won't spend much time on the industrial revolution as I think most of us learned a fair amount about it when we were younger. We know about the smokestacks, the child labour, mass production, and the beginning of workers' rights and unions. What I will spend some time on though, is mass consumerism. It is where we are today.

Mass Consumerism

Consumerism has had different guises. We commonly refer to it as a new thing – it's not. As soon as we had excess, we became consumers, consuming other people's things. First consuming for need, and then for want, which has become the norm. The difference is that now almost everyone in the word is a mass consumer. We've been continually consuming more and more, until we reached mass consumerism, which is what we have today. This really kicked off after the Second World War. Mass production and technology moved us to a new level in production and consumerism. Now we consume more for our 'free time', interests and wants, than we do for our needs – and consumerism drives most economies.

People worked and the more they produced, the more money they had to spend. Kids got paper rounds to save up for a new pair of trendy shoes, drums or a hair dryer while their parents worked overtime to pay for that holiday or went to night school to improve their knowledge and earnings. People had a purpose: to improve the quality of their lives – and they felt valued. While this was not universal, life had been generally improving.

As people earned more, they spent more. One good factory job could support a family of four. As people spent more and populations grew, extra workers were needed and initially high prices on new goods and services dropped due to economies of scale, technology efficiencies, immigrants and globalisation. For those of us that remember, the first CD players cost £1,000 in the mid 1980's, and then they were so cheap they were given away, after which they became obsolete.

When the baby boomers arrived in the 1960's, true mass consumerism exploded. Globally. While the automobile was a central enabler of consumerist growth, the tipping point was 2014 when, for the first time, more of the global population had a mobile phone than didn't. The mobile phone has become a 'must have'. A person sitting in a remote village or town in North America, Europe, Asia or Africa has more horsepower in the palm of their hand than the technology that put us on the moon a mere fifty years ago. Today 69% of the world's population has a mobile phone, from toddler to centenarian, and over 50% of them are smart phones. I saw two young girls in the Atlas Mountains in Morocco watching their herd of sheep, while suitably engrossed on their smart phones. Imagine who and what they could connect to from a remote mountain top. It truly boggles the mind.

As populations grew, new consumers entered the market, which created new demand. This growth in consumer demand also increased the selection available. We have so many choices now on everything, even a cup of coffee. Today, consumer spending in the UK and US are responsible for over 70% of the economy.

Let's put this into perspective. A hundred years ago, a wealthy person would have had no central heating at home or work, probably no electricity, no TV, no warm cars, no oven, no fridge, no fruit year-round. Today, a person living on Level 3 lives better and for longer than the wealthiest people at that time. We did well overall.

For 10,000 years we aspired to produce more, and it paid off, big time, albeit a bit slowly if you measure the progress over 200,000 years. Lucky us!

In the past one hundred years we have produced a great life that can completely take care of every person's basic needs and at a high standard everywhere. Work hard. Produce more. Earn more. Simple and it worked.

We had purpose. Our purpose for 200,000 years has been to survive by producing better. We derived value in ourselves by participating in production. And the population grew.

Over the past one hundred years, population growth created billions of new consumers. Literally millions of new potential customers were being born every day. Demand grew as if by magic. Ever increasing growth, coupled with enhanced production techniques, created economies of scale, which consumers benefitted from. Most daily products have been getting relatively cheaper to purchase. We're getting considerably more bang for our buck now than in 1950. However, some of our costs have risen tremendously since the 80's, the most significant of these being property. This impacts us particularly as we all need a roof over our heads. As the world population grew, demand for property naturally rose, and as people tend to congregate, prices went up in desirable areas. Very simply, as Will Rogers supposedly once said about land, 'they ain't make'n no more of it'.

Don't worry millennials. That only works where demand (the population) keeps growing. Once the population stops growing, or even begins to decrease, the drop in demand will not only keep prices flat, but actually reduce them, as each new build will increase supply without a matching demand. And guess what, you're in luck! The world population is going to stop growing soon. In fact, in most 'developed' countries it already has. If their population is still increasing it is due to immigration.

The main reason the world population is continuing to grow today is because we're living longer. Not because of new births. In 1950 the global life expectancy was forty-five. Today it's seventy-two. Result!!!! We're actually having fewer kids though. Most Western countries, plus Japan and China have a problem with a growth rate of less than one child per person. Bad luck for Japan, which has virtually no immigration and whose population is already shrinking (-500,000 in 2018) and now actually has more homes than people.[16]

It's only immigration that keeps housing demand up.

It turns out that the best contraceptive in the world is rising living standards. As a country creeps up the UN income table, its birth rate drops. The 'better-off' have fewer kids. In 1950 live births were five children per woman, so for simplicity's sake we'll say 2.5 kids per person, to include the men. Globally, right now, it's gone down to 2.5 per woman (that's 1.25 per person) and it's forecast to drop below two live births per woman before the end of the century.

Europe's birth rate is 1.6 and North America's is 1.9. [17] India is at 2.1 and China is at 1.5.[18] We need a birth rate of 2.1 simply to keep the population flat.

Currently, there are about 8 billion[19] of us and according to the UN we're forecast to peak at roughly 11 billion by the end of the century. And then start declining.

While the UN makes this peak population forecast, a growing number of people believe the world population will reach its highest point long before reaching 11 billion. The main reason they cite is that as societies move up the development table and urbanise, women stop having babies. A clear illustration is Empty Planet by two Canadians Darrel Bricker and John Ibbitson.[20] They expect a peak by 2050 at somewhere between 8 to 9 billion people. Others, such as Norwegian Jorgen Randers and Austrian Prof Wolfgang Lutz, who previously worried about over population, now expect a peak of 8 billion in 2040.[21]

What does this mean for the property market? Let's work it out. Let's look globally first. If the UN expects a peak of 11.2 billion people in 2100 and 20% are kids living at home, then we will reach peak property demand at 8.9 billion sometime around 2040.

If construction keeps pace with population growth, when the global population hits 8.9 billion, we'll have all the roofs we need. In fact, demand could decrease each time a new one is added. Watch out house prices.

If the Canadians are right and the population peaks at 9 billion people, and 20% of those are kids living at home, then peak demand for property will be at 7.2 billion – a number we have already surpassed. In fact, this appears to be the case worldwide. Specific regions and specific cities behave differently of course, but the global, easy property boom is over.

Worldwide, there are many places already literally giving away property. Italy, Spain and Portugal, to name a few, are doing this to keep ancient villages alive. Italy was giving them away for $1.[22] Not that $1 is likely to put many people off. Italy is now giving people €700 a month for three years if they move to villages with less than 2,000 people and start business – of any sort.[23] And Japan, which has over 8mn unoccupied properties, is giving them away for free.[24]

So that we're clear, yes - the easy property boom is almost over. The only places where property prices will continue to rise are where there is immigration and migration, which keeps demand up. Take note: UK and US – stop immigration at your peril!

Immigration

The true masters of the universe are immigrants. We're all immigrants or descended from them. Since the beginning of our history, people have moved to greener pastures. Human history is a story of immigration. Most reports and statistics clearly show that immigrants overwhelmingly contribute far more to their host country than they take from it.

Immigrants tend to work harder, cheaper and take jobs that 'locals' no longer wish to do. They're literally 'hungrier' – to a point that some become huge success stories. Or their children do. Immigrants have a very strong work ethic. Immigrants do not immigrate to 'leach' off society, as some right-wingers would have us believe. They risk life and limb to do better, to make something of themselves and their families, to improve their lives. They are important drivers of many economies.

We need immigrants for loads of reasons. They pay tax, which helps the government of course. Can't argue with that – especially as the tax base is getting smaller as people age and retire. Immigrants also tend to be younger, so require fewer social services, such as medical. In fact, many organisations would have a hard time delivering services to us at all, if not for immigrants. Whether they are nurses, doctors, waiters or strawberry pickers, we need immigrants.

The next battle will be for immigrants. As explained, many countries have less than a 2.1 replacement birth rate and we are aging. We won't have enough new taxpayers or nurses – just when we need them most. In the UK, applications to nursing schools have dropped by 12% due to educational costs and poor wages.[25] Meanwhile, 24% are dropping out before completing their studies,[26] and since Brexit there's been a 96% drop in nurses wanting to come to the UK from the EU.[27] There are 107,000 NHS vacancies in the UK and over 40,000 of them are nurses.[28]

Ironically, all those older Brexit voters won't have enough nurses, doctors and NHS staff to take care of them. Talk about cutting off your nose to spite your face.

Germany realises this. It's why they accepted 1 million Syrian refuges in 2016 – refugees who were doctors, teachers, artists, nurses and entrepreneurs. Canada sees it too and wants to attract 1 million immigrants in the next three years.

The world is no longer worried about overpopulation but underpopulation. Underpopulation is very real, a serious worry and a threat to our future.

Underpopulation means fewer young workers, which in turn means less tax revenue and fewer doctors and nurses, just at the same time as there are additional older people not paying tax, but needing doctors, nurses and social services. Globally, we just crossed a major threshold – there are now more people alive over the age of sixty-five, than aged five or younger.[29]

Let's look at some simple stats. No matter which report you read, in all of them, immigrants put far more into the economy than they take out. Let's look at the UK first. One of the rallying cries for leaving the EU is that EU immigrants were coming to the UK to go on benefits. (They can't actually receive benefits until they've paid into the UK system for two years, but that's hardly mentioned). The other claim is that we are throwing money away by making contributions to the EU.

Let's evaluate those statements. In fact, EU migrants made a net contribution of £19.3 billion in 2016. This is better than all the other migrant groups combined, who made a net £7.5 billion contribution. On average, each EU migrant contributes £2,300 more to the UK economy than they receive, while a UK-born person's net contribution is negative - £70.[30]

And of course, there's VAT and how EU migrants support the British economy through purchasing and providing goods and services. These are some serious numbers. Now, how much does the UK pay to the EU each year? Let's see what the UK Office for National Statistics says:

The ONS says the UK pays the EU £20 billion, kind of, as we receive a rebate of £4.5 billion straight back. Then, the UK public sector receives £4.5 billion back. And then, the UK private sector receives another £1.1 billion. So, the actual UK contribution to the EU is £9.9 billion.[31]

EU Payments	billions £	
Total Due	£20.0	
Rebate		£4.5
Public sector		£4.5
Private sector		£1.1
Total paid to the EU	£9.9	

How much did we say EU immigrants contribute each year? Oh yeah, £19.3 billion.

Annual contribution to the UK economy

	billions £
EU migrants	£19.3
Other migrants	£7.5
Total	**£26.8**

As an aside, second generation immigrants also contribute more to the economy than those who are third generation or more.

£19.3 billion inflow minus £9.9 billion outflow means that the UK treasury benefits by £9.4 billion each year from being in the EU and allowing immigrants in.

Total EU Costs & Benefits	billions £	
Total paid to the EU	£9.9	
EU Migrant tax		£19.3
Gain to the UK		**£9.4**

Here's the real zinger though, Bloomberg Economics worked out that Brexit, by the end of 2019, had already cost the UK more than all its payments to the EU budget over the past forty-seven years. That's over £130 billion. And the UK hadn't even left yet.[32]

Of course, then there are all the other benefits for business of being part of the largest single market in the world. Plus, all the personal and cultural advantages, but we're just looking at immigrants right now.

The US paints a similar story to the UK. Undocumented workers contribute $11.6 billion a year to America in taxes – but they can't receive anything back as they are in the country illegally.[33] In 2014 immigrants paid $328 billion in local, state and federal taxes. In California their contribution was more than a quarter of all the tax the state received, while in New York and New Jersey, it was almost a quarter of all taxes both those states received.[34] Like the UK, they also spend money on local goods and services as well providing them. It's worth noting that California's economy is roughly the size of the UK economy (a tad bigger).

Immigrants are clearly a significant part of the tax base and provide services we need and want. We need immigrants.

The last land grab is on, and it's not for land. It's for people – for immigrants. But this won't go on indefinitely.

Globalisation

The term 'globalisation' is thrown around quite a bit. But what is it and what does it mean to us? When we hear the word 'globalisation' some of us think about losing jobs to low wage countries. Jobs are a part of globalisation, but it's far, far more than just that. Look around where you're sitting right now. Start with your mobile. Where is it made? Who thought of it? Where was it designed? Its components, the minerals, come from different parts of the world. Various constituents were assembled in different places. Final assembly could have been in multiple places as well. And it could be sold anywhere in the world and bought by anyone. Your phone was made as efficiently and cheaply as possible using resources from around the world.

This is globalisation.

Tens, if not hundreds, of countries, companies and people were involved in producing your iPhone. From the US and the EU for design, to Mongolia and Africa for resources; and from Korea, Japan and Taiwan for glass and processors, to China for completion. All of them were working for your benefit, keeping costs down and quality up. Lots of people around the world were involved in the process of creating, producing, marketing and distributing your iPhone. It was a global effort.

This is globalisation. And you benefit from it every day.

It's the shirt on your back at an affordable price, the shoes on your feet, your fridge, your car. It's also your music, your films, your holidays, your colleagues, your friends and your family. We live in a global world, which has benefitted us all. Some more so than others, however living conditions for the developed and developing world are generally much, much better than they were seventy years ago. Life is awesome for many. We're lucky compared to previous generations.

Back to jobs — that's yesterday's battle — although there never really was one. Globalisation isn't taking jobs, machines are. The jobs' landscape changed. The types of jobs in different countries simply changed. It's gone on since the beginning of time, albeit at a slower pace. As low-level manufacturing jobs went to low wage countries, new jobs were created in high wage countries. Often they were service jobs. We used to make things. Then, we switched to providing services. This was good for both types of country, for the person who got the new job in the 'outsourced' (low wage) country and for the person who lost their old job, if they found another sort of job in the high wage country.

However, those jobs are gone, and they aren't coming back. In fact, while jobs keep moving to cheaper places they are also simultaneously becoming more automated. The whole world has the same problem: jobs will go to where that given task can be performed most efficiently — and we all benefit. The jobs battle is not about jobs going to other people. It's about losing jobs to technology and automation. That's the job killer — computing power plus automation plus artificial intelligence. Manufacturing as a share of GDP in the US and UK are both at their highest in decades — but with fewer workers. And now services are being automated.

US manufacturing
Rebased (1980 = 100)

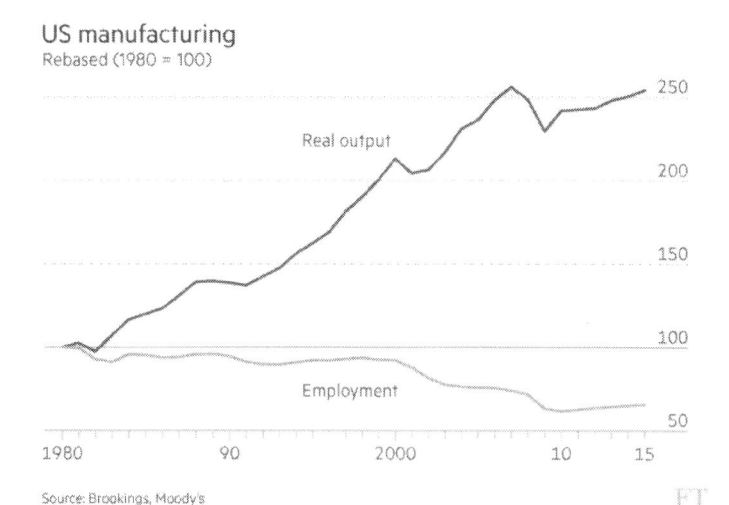

Real output / Employment chart, 1980–2015, Source: Brookings, Moody's

One of the problems of efficiency, by its nature, is the minimisation or complete removal of people from processes. This is how we become more efficient today, by removing people from the equation. We reduce costs and one of those costs is people. People are viewed as an expense to be negated and we can never improve our efficiency as much as a computer can.

But hang on – it also benefits us, right? Availability of cheaper and better products and services means better lifestyles. It's a double-edged sword, but only because we look at it in the same way we always have. The world has developed, and people have justified their existence, by producing things they could sell, so they could in turn consume things they needed, and then wanted.

This process has become extremely efficient and is becoming even more so as more is automated. In many ways you could say that up until now, humankind was focused on taking care of daily needs, but in the developed world, we can technically supply food shelter and clothing for everyone now. Technology has played a key role in this from the beginning of time. From agriculture, to manufacturing, to automation, technology has played a key part in our evolution. In each technology shift the lower wage people lost out and new people (and countries) became wealthy, if their timing was right. Jobs, particularly physical ones, were lost downstream while new jobs were created upstream.

Automation has now reached a point though where it's taking not just blue-collar 'physical' jobs, but it's creeping upstream into the professions' white-collar 'mind' jobs.

Accountants and lawyers are next. Jobs with a repetitive element are in the firing line and artificial intelligence is pushing these boundaries. Accountancy software, that takes the digital data from each transaction and compiles and electronically files all the necessary reporting, means less demand for accountants. No longer do people show up at accountants' offices with a box full of receipts once a year. Rather, they use services such as FreeAgent and Xero, for $20 a month.

Lawyers used to write contracts, each one from scratch, first by hand, then on a typewriter. Initially, they fought against templates when computers first appeared. Let's be honest, how many different employment contracts or apartment rental contracts are there? Only a few details need adding or changing. Now there are literally hundreds of websites with prewritten, template contracts for just about everything, their cost – free to $35 a year.

Globalisation is not the job killer. Automation is. What are we to do?

AI (Artificial Intelligence)

At this point, Artificial Intelligence (AI) needs a closer look because this is an area where, if we don't get our proverbial sh*t together, we can kiss our proverbial ass**s goodbye. I'm not even going to try to address all the moral and philosophical questions that Machine Learning (ML) and AI raise. That's a whole other thing. But I do believe we should 'find ourselves' and quickly, so that we at least know what we are and what we want.

ML and AI are similar-ish and often mixed up. For our purposes we'll refer to them collectively as AI and we don't need to spend time on the difference, but here's a quick explanation for the curious:

What most people think is AI, is actually ML. ML learns, AI does, and it follows instructions like algorithms. Let's say we put up a picture of ten sets of traffic lights. Then we put up a picture of one set that has a red lamp and an orange lamp but is missing one lamp. If you asked ML what the other lamp colour should be, it would answer green. It can figure it out. AI couldn't figure it out. AI would only know the answer if you had previously told it that those three colours make up a traffic light or given it a set of rules to work it out.

The first thing to note here is that ML and AI are ending the manufacturing and the automobile revolutions. They are almost over as we know them. The jobs are going and will soon be gone forever. Self-driving electronic cars and trucks (*autopods*) produced and serviced by automated technology will mean no more truck drivers, taxi drivers, pizza delivery people or petrol station attendants. Fewer mechanics will be needed as the *pods* will self-diagnose and not break down as often. And if they do, they will plug themselves into more technology to be diagnosed. And then, many repairs will be done electronically and robotically.

It will be a world with no more MOT's, servicing, speeding tickets or council parking fees. What will local government do about this loss of income? How will they replace it? How will councils pay for the services they must still supply?

We need to decide what kind of world we want before we can figure out the boundaries of AI. Where do people, us, fit into the future? What do we want to do when we get up in the morning? What is important to us? Why do we exist? What is our purpose? Our value? What makes us different to AI? What is the USP (Unique Selling Point) of the human race, the USP of earth?

It's probably easier to see if we don't overthink it.

We have feelings, emotions and compassion. We have senses. AI has sensors. We figure shit out. AI computes it.

Sure, it can appear that AI has emotions as it learns and mimics, but the difference is that AI makes *decisions*, while people make *choices*. Of course, we also make decisions, and AI keeps beating us at those. But many of our decisions are choices. AI can't choose, it can *only* decide. Nor would we want AI to choose. But in future… it could become sentient.

Think of it this way. Someone has pain. We think it's real and react accordingly. We feel sympathy. We feel empathy, well, most of us do. An AI or ML bot (short for robot) could be taught to read those emotions and display sympathy as well, but they wouldn't feel it. AI and ML wouldn't be able to empathise. They are not truly sympathising. They are making output decisions based on the input – display sympathy. If AI were told that pain was good and to express laughter when they encountered it, they would. If we showed ML pictures of people in pain with everyone laughing then it would learn to laugh as well. AI and ML are what we tell them to be – for now.

We make choice decisions all the time, from what colour socks or shirt to wear, to which university to attend, job to take, film to watch, or favourite painting. We make choices because of how we 'feel', like, 'What do I feel like eating today?' plus practicality. If you're going somewhere cold, most likely you won't take shorts, but not necessarily. We make a choice decision. When we suddenly decide to take the long way home through the park on a sunny day, we make a choice, a gut feeling sometimes. It might be longer, but that's NOT what's important at that time.

Sometimes those choices turn out well, sometimes they don't. Sometimes they go in our favour, yet we achieve little, sometimes they go wrong, yet we achieve much, by accident, or perhaps because we tried with an open mind. We learn from our choices.

These feelings translate into choice decisions that define us, who we are, what we feel and how we interact with the world. Feelings are analogue. AI is digital. It's not real. We'd do well to remember this. And if we don't get it right now, what happens when AI goes organic and becomes live?

AI is great for making decisions where little subjectivity is required. AI can search and analyse heaps of data far faster than people ever can, and it can achieve quicker results. From a safety perspective, it's a no-brainer. AI is great. It can 'learn' from what it does and teach itself. It starts to get kind of scary though, when we introduce one AI to another, and they begin to develop their own language, as happened in 2017 at Facebook – and it's normal.[35] Think about that for a moment. The AI did this for practical purposes, the AI decided it was more expedient for them to communicate this way, and Facebook only found out by accident. And AI has now been taught to design its own AI chips, and it does it better than we can.[36] Which means even many physicists and rockets scientists could be out of a job. Like I said, AI is working its way upstream and no one is safe.

This then begs the question of course, at what point do humans and the environment (earth) not seem necessary to the AI bots?

We are understandably nervous about AI, and the thought of AI making subjective decisions, objectively, makes us truly apprehensive. There's no compassion. No love. AI is one of the biggest choice decisions humanity has ever had to make and how we survive will depend on those choices. Rather than making them based on today's reality, we should first imagine what we want tomorrow's world to look like? Do we want it to be ours still? Can it be?

It can be. It must be. AI can play a very strong role in 'producing' needed and wanted things, and to help us deliver good quality services. It can help us have an infrastructure that meets the aspirations of the human race, but let's keep AI in the objective decisions arena. Not subjective choices.

Let's limit its scope of influence. Let's keep final choices analogue. Let's teach AI that analogue is the most valuable thing in the world. Let AI know that people and the environment are what are truly valuable.

How do we do that? Focus.

As with anything that learns, the objective is the same, improvement. Our quest for learning creates competition, which creates more choices and better results. AI is the same; it is seeking to improve by learning. That's its strength, which is also as scary as hell. It would seem to me that the smart thing to do is keep AI very task focused, let it learn how to do one thing really well – open heart surgery for instance, with all its learning focused on better learning, and delivering one objective. But if there's a choice with subjective elements to be made, during surgery, for example, a human surgeon needs to make the call.

AI must value that it can't make subjective decisions, only a human can.

Here's an interesting example of choices that are subjective and cultural but affect self-driving cars. In the case of an impending accident, who do you save? It's called 'the trolley problem'.[37]

The choice of *who* the car hits or saves, is actually a very difficult question. It's a moral question. Do you save the people in the car or the pedestrians? And what about older or younger people? Millions of people in two hundred and thirty-three countries made 400 million choices related to this and the answers varied considerably from culture to culture with an East-West divide. The West saved the young. The East saved the old. The West leaned towards saving more lives instead of *who* the people were, while the Japanese saved the passenger, because the pedestrians were jay walking.[38]

Think about this: a Chinese AI, capable of subjective, cultural decision-making, would save an adult Chinese party member over a child, whereas in the UK it would be the opposite. What happens if you import a Chinese car or are driving in China, or vice versa? Or what if you moved to the US and imported your Chinese car?

Then, imagine political beliefs. What if the AI knows you're a Conservative or a Liberal? Does it decide based on the driver's choices or the person who 'programmed' it or the government? And, remember, AI learns. So, we're teaching AI our morals – whatever they may be.

As important as our decision-making processes are our emotional processes. AI cannot be allowed to encroach on this world, the feeling world. Humans should teach and use AI, but not let it choose.

A clear indication of the direction we're heading in, if we don't wake up, is the electronic babysitters we can now provide for our children. We've reached a point where an AI bot can be seen as a 'friend' to our children. And more. The 2015 TV series *Humans* offers a glimpse of the kind of things we could expect in the not too distant future.[39] The housebound with limited mobility and the elderly in need of human interaction, may also find some meaning in interaction with robot carers. But, robot babysitters and companions on a global scale would lead to the further disconnect of many people from real human interaction. We don't want that.

The Environment

The environment is not well. This is crucial. We know we're destroying it and we need to urgently do something about it. It's the golden goose, yet we're killing it, and potentially ourselves, through abuse and taking it for granted. Clearly, we need to value it, and the human lives that depend on it, much more.

Many of us love going to the beach or spending a warm afternoon beside a river or lake. We like walking through the countryside and breathing clean air. We like nature. We take it for granted. But the environment is a critical issue.

When temperatures swing wildly day-to-day, and we get a month's rain in one hour, and hurricanes get stronger, and there are plastic islands the size of a country floating around, we start to realise something's wrong.

Most of us agree it got this way so quickly because we've not been paying close enough attention to the damage we've been doing. We've been taking from nature without giving enough thought to the impact our activities are having on the environment.

The reason this happened is simple. Money. It wasn't in our financial interest. Companies wanted to keep costs down, so they took from nature what they wanted, with no regard for the future. We, as consumers, went along with this because we didn't want to pay higher prices either. We all created the problem and now we all need to work towards fixing it.

Without a healthy environment the human race is doomed. Companies and people do and will continue to take things that are 'free' and not ascribe any value to them. This has happened with the environment. This needs to change.

Right now, it's often cheaper to buy a new product than fix an old one. Companies will only be motivated to make things with longer lives, and consumers will only demand them, if they need to pay for the environmental impact.

It's cheaper now to throw away old phones or washing machines, than fix them when they break. Technology is difficult to recycle and lots of minerals are used in its manufacture, so the environmental impact is huge. If there were more realistic charges for the use of the environment – at extraction and at disposal – then manufacturers would be motivated to make more modular and repairable products, as it would keep their costs down.

It's not just about how we're destroying the environment, it's also about how we're losing touch with it. There are many people who've never seen a real cow or a chicken. They've not had the pleasure of wandering through nature and appreciating it. Children need to be introduced to its value so that it becomes a part of their psyche. People who have grown up around nature rarely cease to respect and enjoy it. It's therapeutic. It calms us. It's good for the soul and it puts us back in touch with the analogue world around us.

Let's not forget space. It too is part of our environment and it's actually getting dangerous out there because millions of pieces of space garbage are floating around – and there have already been collisions.[40] Throwing a satellite away is no different from throwing a plastic bottle away – it's just a lot bigger. [41] We need to stop littering in space.[42]

Until now, we have 'developed' and people have lived better by taking advantage of the environment with no regard to cost. Those days are over. If we don't act responsibly now, Mother Nature will bite us in the ass. She's already slapping us around quite a bit. The environment is analogue; it's real, as we are. It bleeds, as we do. It's not artificial bits and bytes. We are part of a giant living analogue system. This is what we are. We need to take care of it. The environment is humankind's most valuable asset and it belongs to us all.

Come on, unless you're really, really clocked out you know we have a major problem with the way we've abused the environment and where it's headed. The reason for this is simple. It was 'free'. And no one wants to pay the price now. I said that earlier, so just let me refocus that: the vested interests don't want to pay the price of having to reinvent themselves. They've got a cash cow and they want it to remain that way. Whether their trade involves oil, fracking or plastic. Instead of being leaders and pushing into new ways of delivering eco-friendly services, packaging and goods, many companies just want to hold on to what they have now, with no regard to tomorrow.

World temperatures are at all time average highs, ice caps are melting, and the air is dirty, yet many of the super-rich choose to ignore this and some even mock people who are trying to make a difference and save the planet. July 2019 was the hottest month globally since records began,[43] Canada's permafrost is melting seventy years earlier than expected[44] and Siberia is on fire.[45] Let's not forget the Amazon over the summer of 2019 and the fires in Australia, which began in December 2019 and are still continuing in January 2020. As I write, 18 million acres have already been scorched in Australia (an area larger than Belgium and Denmark combined) and in New South Wales (NSW) alone, more than 3,000 homes have been destroyed.[46]

Earth is Heating Up

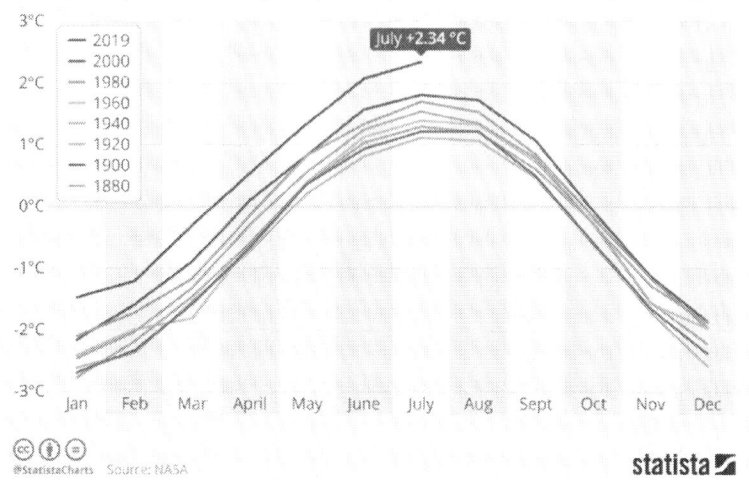

Monthly divergence from average temperature (calculated for 1980-2015), by selected years

[Chart showing temperature divergence by month for years 1880, 1900, 1920, 1940, 1960, 1980, 2000, 2019. July 2019: +2.34 °C]

Source: NASA

statista

Greta Thunberg came to the world's attention as a young activist who protested that her generation's future was being seriously threatened by global climate change. She and the 1.4 million students, who joined her from one hundred and twelve countries around the world in March 2019, know this is serious. Thurnberg is motivating people as Severn Cullis-Suzuki did in 1992 when, at the age of 12, she addressed the Earth Summit in Rio de Janeiro.[47] Over twenty years later Suzuki is still an environmental activist – amongst other things – but still nowhere enough has been done since her speech. We weren't listening. We need to this time.

But the super-rich don't appear to care. As an example, one need look no further than Arron Banks, insurance mogul and founder of Leave.Eu (pro Brexit). He replied as follows to a tweet from Caroline Lucas, leader of the UK Green Party to sixteen-year-old environmental activist, Greta Thunberg, who was sailing rather than flying to the UN in New York to ensure she had a zero-carbon footprint:

> **Arron Banks**
> @Arron_banks
>
> Freak yachting accidents do happen in August ...
>
> > **Caroline Lucas** @CarolineLucas · Aug 14
> >
> > Bon voyage to @GretaThunberg for her 2-week zero-carbon trip by sail across the North Atlantic
> >
> > She's carrying the vital message to the UN that time is running out to address the #ClimateEmergency
>
> 10:11 PM · Aug 14, 2019 · Twitter for iPhone
>
> **429** Retweets **2.7K** Likes

We should all be applauding Greta for her efforts.

Don't think it's just about banning plastic straws and plastic bags either. It's the whole environment. The UN knows it as well and in August 2019 published a scary report about the effect humans are having on the environment.[48] We need to urgently pay attention.

It's time for governments to acknowledge this and do something about it. It's time for universities, whose scientists know full well the irreversible damage we are doing, to join Thunberg's protest. It's about time we made real changes to our lives, even if it's difficult. This is our 'green evolution', which we ignore at our peril.

Politics and Politicians

Politics has existed since we lived in small groups in caves. Someone would always be vying to be in charge and then would lead us into battle with other groups to acquire their goods and yes, their women.

We don't trust them because they say one thing and do another. We feel that many have never worked a 'real' job, and most are from privileged backgrounds. We have a complicated relationship with them. This is because our expectations don't reflect reality. Think for a moment about what a politician's actual job is.

Most people will say that politicians are there to do what the people want, to look out for the best interests of the voters.

They're not. The job of a politician is to get elected. It's simple. If they don't get elected, they don't have a job.

From the get-go, this poses a problem. Think about adults and children, say five and six-year-old children, maybe your children. They may want to stay up late playing on their tablets, rather than going to bed and sleeping, but that's not good for them. Against their wishes, you read them a story and put them to bed. Initially, they didn't want to do this, but they end up enjoying the book and your time together. You are helping create a better human being. Everyone benefits. But your children didn't want this initially and complained about having to go to bed. If you'd had a vote about going to bed you'd have lost. Thankfully, they don't have a vote on sleep time, yet. But it highlights the point that we must often make decisions people don't like at the time, yet in the long run, it's for the best.

So, should a politician do what they think is best for the citizens – even if it means losing the election and power – or should they do what the citizens *want*?

Well, consider this: we're missing the bigger point. A politician's number one job is to get elected, plain and simple. No 'ifs' or 'buts' about it. Their job is to win elections.

The reality is that most US and UK politicians these days, are wealthy. Over half are multi-millionaires before joining government and many attended private schools. Their salaries and perks aren't too bad either. In the UK, MP's earn £75,000 from their government salaries (plus many benefits). This is more than 90% of the rest of the country.[49] US politicians are no better. Their median net worth is $1.1 million (excluding houses)[50] and they pay themselves $174,000 a year, which is more than what 95% of the rest of the country earn. And these are the people who 'represent the country'.

Some politicians gain followers by rallying people behind their beliefs. Most do it by attempting to say what they think the voters want to hear – promising anything to get into power. That's why they waffle, don't give direct answers to questions, or simply lie, which seems to be quite popular at the moment. This is not to suggest that all politicians are tarred with the same brush. Thankfully, we have the Kenneth Clarkes, Elizabeth Warrens, Alexandria Ocasio-Cortezs and Obamas who talk straight. But, on the other hand, we have the Theresa Mays, Donald Trumps and Boris Johnsons who will say and do almost anything to hold on to power.

Incidentally, I find many ex-Prime Ministers and ex-Presidents far more honest and interesting after they've left politics, when they are more likely to be open and free to give straight answers, whereas live politics seems to stifle truth.

Pesky financial backers further complicate the matter. In order to attract voters, politicians need money to campaign with. To win elections politicians need to keep voters and financial backers happy. Or at least promise to. They need to keep both groups happy. This can be a delicate balancing act as often voters and financial backers want different things.

No wonder most people are wary of politicians.

It would be great to create a new hybrid system. Something like the good points about the Supreme Court in the US and the House of Lords (the non-hereditary part) in the UK. Both groups consider issues intelligently, discuss them, research them and do what they think is best. They can do this because they don't have an electorate to please. They aren't up for re-election.

Now, how to choose them? Perhaps they could have maximum fixed terms?

Let's face it, the very word 'politics' conjures up bad thoughts. People groan when they hear the words 'office politics'. Most people don't think of 'politics' of any sort, as good or constructive.

Here's what 'politics' means in the dictionary:

- Use of intrigue or strategy in obtaining any position of power or control, as in business, university, etc

And if that isn't enough on our plates already, we must also contend with the rise of the right wing that pretend none of the issues facing us exist. No bones about it, we are in a moment of massive upheaval in society. We've seen it before and thought, believed, hoped, we'd never see it again – the rise of the far right and dictators, none of whom have been elected by the majority of their populations, but rather, have acquired power through the manipulation of democracy and nationalism – always a dangerous combination.

So, we have Trump in the USA, who openly says he wants to get rid of fixed term limits and claims the 'people' will demand it. There's also Putin in Russia and Xi Jinping in China. After meeting Xi Jinping, who removed China's two-term limit in 2018, Trump showed his support for the idea saying:

"He's now president for life. President for life. No, he's great. And look, he was able to do that. I think it's great. Maybe we'll have to give that a shot some day." [51]

In January 2020, Putin essentially made himself ruler for life. Then, of course, there's Kim Jong-un in North Korea, Jair Bolsonaro in Brazil, and Boris Johnson in the UK. The list goes on and includes the leaders of many African nations, the Middle East and Asia. The only thing any of these people care about is power. They don't care about their populations. And yes, this even includes the ex-Labour leader Jeremy Corbyn in the UK. The reason Corbyn wanted out of the European Union (EU) was so that he could do whatever he wanted in the UK, unhindered by the EU, while blaming the Conservatives for leaving the EU. Look at how he runs the labour party with his Momentum group, in which there is no room for dissent. Corbyn appears to be an old-fashioned command and control guy in socialist's clothing.

And there is an unspoken understanding that many of the extreme right have a potential for violence, especially when stirred up by narcissist politicians. When the UK's Boris Johnson said those opposed to him and Brexit were 'collaborating with the enemy'[52] (our friends in the EU) he's fanning the flames of hate. His language is that of war.

When Trump refused to condemn the violence and murders committed in Charlottesville, Virginia by people carrying Nazi flags and instead said: 'I think there is blame on both sides'[53] he was giving fringe alt-right (extreme right) people a green light. White supremacists are killing people, murdering politicians (like Jo Cox in the UK) and beating up and threatening journalists while calling them unpatriotic. These people are terrorists, but as long as some politicians are refusing to call them this or bring them to heel, they think their behaviour is acceptable. These politicians are fanning the flames of the far right as it helps their agenda.

Unfortunately, politics sucks. But we need government.

The Generational Split

There are always generational splits. Even though the same issues affect the young and the old, they are felt differently. But now, perhaps what separates the generations is more a gulf than a split.

The two major impacts are automation and value.

The older generation (35+) still believe in producing things to make them feel of value. They want a job. The younger generation is confused and feels ripped off by the older generation.

Truth be told, we are all a bit confused about what exactly we should be producing at the moment. It's not clear where we're going, and we need to sort out some hairy problems. Thing is, we don't need more production now. Instead, we need more 'supporting' roles. These are roles we haven't previously valued as much as they don't immediately 'produce'. But they are socially valuable. Doctors, nurses, teachers, caregivers, social workers, hospitals, schools and nursing homes are what we need, as well as artists and musicians. Unfortunately, we view these occupations as unproductive and costly because they don't make things to consume, even though they do make healthy consumers.

Production is what we, as a society, have positively valued and it's how the GDP balance sheet has been computed. Problem is, what we measured and valued yesterday is not fit for purpose for today and tomorrow.

It's not simply about production anymore. We need to understand this and accept that the primary motivators that have fuelled our development to this point are no longer the primary objective. AI and automation can provide much of this. Thus, what we value needs to change. To date we rewarded production, what now?

As reward for production diminishes, angst naturally arises. We must counter this by finding something new to reward. We must evolve.

Current Trends

In the countries where Level 4, in the Gapminder Income Levels definitions, is the norm and often referred to as 'the West', we are seeing a lot of angst with a few major themes arising in each group, although, Scandinavian countries are a slight exception.

1. People in Group 4, and to a degree group 3, are complaining about the ever-widening gap between the rich and the middle classes. Yes, the middle classes, not the poor.
2. Groups 1, 2 and 3 are still dealing with corruption, which is largely responsible for stopping progress through to group 4.
3. Politicians everywhere have lost the trust of the people they are supposed to represent. Voters are frustrated.
4. Group 4 infrastructure is not meeting the demands of people.
5. Group 4 social services are being weakened.
6. Group 4 is seeing an increase in anxiety and other depression related situations in younger people, aged twenty-seven and below in particular.
7. Group 4 suicides are higher than any other group.

Since the focus of this book is Level 4, we'll address them primarily. There are two recent events in the UK and US that highlight the differences today across many of the group 4 societies – the clashes between the far right and liberalism, and the young and old.

Brexit and Trump are two hugely divisive issuers. And there is no fence sitting. You're either on one side or the other. It's a right vs. left, isolationist vs. global, liberal vs. hard right. Let's look at them a bit closer: Brexit voters in the UK and Trump voters in the US have much in common, including that inside each group there are two similar sub-groups.

White people who are 50+ tend to be pro Trump and pro Brexit while younger people are overwhelmingly against both – the younger, the more so.

Let's look at pro Brexit and pro Trump people first. On the one hand, there are those that believe that opportunity has left them behind. They used to be primarily 'blue collar' workers but are increasingly being joined by mid-level 'white collar' workers. Their old jobs have disappeared, and their new ones don't pay as much. The cost of living is always increasing and social services, their safety net, feel like they're being dismantled. They see fewer opportunities for their children. They are desperate for change and a chance to contribute, to get up in the morning and have a purpose, to add value and to feel respected. They don't want to hear about LGBTQ rights or bans on plastic, which they feel are today's liberal talking points. They want to return to the 'good ol' days' when their purpose was to earn their daily crust by producing. By working. They are dissatisfied. They want and deserve respect. They need purpose and value and the right job will give them this.

They feel no one listens to them anymore; no one understands their problems. And they're right. We haven't been listening or understanding. Well intentioned 'liberals' must be able to know what the problem is before they can attempt to solve it; they need to recognise that the issue here is the sense of lack of value due to lack of purpose. It's not just a tin of beans or a roof over their heads this group lacks.

Then, there are the inward looking, upper middle classes and the wealthy, the better off 20%. They are predominantly older. They have what they need and want to keep it that way. They have done well for themselves and want to remain in control. These are primarily white and middle-aged or older men and women. They want as few other people having a say in their lives and as little intrusion from the rest of society as possible. They believe they earned what they have and deserve it. Many have worked hard for what they have. They feel valuable. Anyone can have a good life, after all. They feel they have lots of value, more than others. First among equals.

This wealthy group manipulates the 'blue collar' group by promoting the idea that it is the big state, immigrants and politicians that are preventing them from having purpose and value.

The white and wealthy listened to the blue-collar workers and relentlessly targeted anti-government and anti-immigrant messages at them. They were convinced that politicians had let their jobs be snatched by immigrants or sent abroad – that globalisation had taken away their value. Phrases like 'bring it local again', 'regain control', 'make us great again' have promoted this way of thinking among the blue-collar group. They now believe that if they have these jobs back all will be well, Social Services will be able to cope, and they can go back to 'the good ol' days'. Everyone can prosper after-all. The wealthy listened and fanned the flames – and the blue and white-collar groups became one.

CNN commentator, Van Jones said on the 2016 election night in the US, 'this was a whitelash against a changing country.'[54] It's the same with Brexit voters. 'Brexiters' still think Britain is a white colonial power. The words and actions of Trump, and Brexit leaders and supporters, have highlighted that racism is not over.

Of course, it was all a big lie. Blue-collar jobs went because of progress, as many have before. As we already know, manufacturing output has been growing, even in Western countries, but fewer people are required to produce. The wealthy are selling blue-collar people yesterday's dream – a dream that has come and gone, first through mechanisation, then through computers, and now through AI, and the jobs market has changed accordingly. Meanwhile, AI and further automation are creeping up the food chain quickly. Whereas other jobs created new jobs, AI takes no prisoners. It's impacting 'professional' jobs as well now and will continue to do so at an increasing rate.

In a nutshell, the wealthy are selling yesterday, to protect today, and are not thinking about tomorrow.

Now let's look at the other side of the coin, those who voted against Trump and Brexit, the so-called 'liberals'. As a group they can be split into people older or younger than thirty-five.

Those thirty-five plus, although well intentioned, did not realise the extent of blue-collar dis-satisfaction. Their lives are fairly OK. They own their own homes; they may be upper middle class or wealthy as well. They have jobs. They have purpose and value. They also know things can be much better and wish they could fix them. They often feel helpless to make change quickly enough. They see things across the board, as a general state of society, jobs, environment, health care, rights etc. They see people globally and deserving of opportunity and care. They want to protect the weak and to help. Many in this group had 'Saturday jobs' as teenagers and felt they had opportunities.

But, the big underlying problem is that while liberals were focused on rights, and services for all, and the benefits of globalisation, they did not see how blue-collar people were feeling disconnected and disenfranchised. Even though they wanted to do right by them. Most of us missed the recent creeping changes that have negatively affected blue-collar people's sense of personal value. Now we've all heard.

All this is extremely divisive and has hurt families and friends. It's literally tearing our countries apart.

David Cameron was a first-class fool, no pun intended. He thought he would end a long fought internal Conservative party battle by having a referendum on the EU. He gambled and lost. While that's bad enough, he didn't even have the nous to make sure the referendum needed a 60% or 65% majority to pass, as is the expected standard.

Let's look at the Brexit referendum and US Election voting stats. They clearly illustrate the divide on both sides. Brexit 'passed' 51.9% to 48.1%.[55] If you had a show of hands vote, you wouldn't even be able to tell who won. In fact, you couldn't do a show of hands with ten people (six to four) and you'd be hard pressed to see who won with a show of hands with 100 or 100,000 hands.

To further compound things, the 'leave' voters were primarily older, while the 'remain' voters were primarily younger. Two years after the referendum, if you recounted the votes, excluding older voters who died, 'remain' would have won. And new young voters are 82% in favour of remaining. And this is *their future.*

Simple demographics means that 'remain' voters grow by about a quarter of a million a year, while 'leave' voters die by about a third of a million a year.[56] Older people making decisions for the next generation, on a razor thin margin, that has now disappeared, is bound to cause issues. Saturday January 19, 2019 was the crossover date where 'remain' overtook 'leave' – without a single person changing their minds. It means the 'will of the people' has now flipped, even based on the 2016 referendum, and arguably, even despite the result of the 2019 election.

In the US the will of the people was ignored. Trump lost the popular vote to Clinton by 2.9 million votes: 48.2% to Clinton vs. 46.1% to Trump.[57] Trump won the Electoral College to become President. That's why he cannot say that he is the President of the people. The people did not vote Trump in, yet he represents them. The UK is no better. The Conservatives won 365 of 650 seats in Parliament in December 2019, so are calling it a landslide. It's not though as those numbers are wonky due to the rigged 'first past the post' voting system in the UK. It's not proportional representation. The Conservatives took control of the government by winning 56% of the parliamentary seats. But, the Conservatives only won 43.6% of the actual vote. Meaning that 56.4% of the country voted against the Conservatives and against leaving the EU.[58] This is simply not right in all ways.

The current political situations in the UK and the US are a mess and have truly split both countries.

Can't Get No…

… Satisfaction. Now we come to people aged thirty-five and under. Some appear unhappy and lost. This younger group is best exemplified by those in their early to mid-twenties. Bear in mind that what they are feeling and experiencing will apply even more so for the millennials, who are just behind them.

Most have grown up in environments that were Levels 3 and 4. They grew up with smart phones, foreign holidays, education, health care and pocket money. For many, if they had a 'Saturday job', it was extra money, to be used, not for basic necessities, but for other fun things, often experiences.

These young adults care about others, about people's rights and the environment, and because the Internet, technology and travel are so much a part of their lives, they see things globally. They have things in common with people like themselves around the world and feel connected to them.

They see that there are many people with different interests, and they respect this. They believe people have a right to be themselves and love watching others being themselves. Acceptance and individuality rule. They are tolerant. They are thoughtful and caring. They are wonderful. But they are not satisfied.

So many kids and young adults today want to create the next huge app or have a following that is large enough to make money, but that's not where it's at.

Don't get me wrong, there's money to be made from being watched, and it is many a young person's dream. For the few that manage to attract a following, it can be lucrative. A person with 'followers' feels valued and often earns money. They are aspirational. People want to be them. They believe anyone can do it. You just need to get out there. Find an angle, a USP. You are selling yourself and hoping to derive value from it. You need a following. A following is what makes you feel valuable. It's not just about money. They want this, sure. But having 'followers' gives them purpose and intrinsic value. How many people 'liked' your comment or photo is important. It makes you feel as though you have value.

Those aged thirty-five plus have on the one hand created a wonderful environment for their kids. One with quality food, shelter and clothing, mobiles phones and travel, and the newly sought-after thing – experiences. But, it's a life that doesn't give the young many chances to add value, to be of value, to have purpose. The young suffer anxiety because of this lack of purpose. They feel there is little opportunity and worry that coupled with high property prices, they will not even be able live in, let alone own, their own home.

I was visiting a friend recently who had a step rubbish bin under his kitchen counter. He explained that the lid kept hitting the bottom of the counter and making a noise. So he fixed the problem. He got some foam and stuck it to the bottom of the kitchen counter in a way that couldn't be seen. Now when he puts his foot down, there is no noise. No thud. And he says sometimes, when he walks by, he steps on the bin purely for the satisfaction of it. Here is a gentle reminder of value that my friend has created. He wanted to beat the problem, to find a solution. So, he did. It was small, but important. Many younger people today would simply buy a new bin and miss out on the feeling of satisfaction and accomplishment that comes with attaining a goal. Much of their lives is like this.

Most people over thirty-five have experienced these feelings of satisfaction. Whether fixing a flat, repairing a garment, putting up shelves or assembling IKEA furniture, saving to buy an album or drum kit or stopping a table from wobbling, we've all been there. We felt great when we accomplished our goals, our purpose. No matter how small. The greater the sacrifice, the more valuable we felt when we accomplished our goal. We had big goals and lots and lots of little ones. We had purpose, and accomplishing those purposes gave us value and pleasure.

Not so for most Level 4 kids. They don't get the satisfaction derived from little accomplishments as they don't need or want to do them, nor do they have an interest in doing them. They don't appreciate the value of these little accomplishments that drive and delight us. This means they also miss out the all-important experience of feeling good about themselves, through seeing the fruits of their labour. They miss the satisfaction of accomplishment. An extreme of this can be seen in school sports days and competitions where some adults thought it would be better if there were no winners, as they didn't want losers. But guess what, everyone loses. This lack of satisfaction is, I believe, one of the causes of anxiety today in the young. And it's because of us, their parents, and society. We thought we were doing the right thing – we weren't.

Let's look at how that manifests itself on a day-to-day basis. Kids and young adults today say they want things to change, but they generally don't do anything about it. They often claim they can't make any changes and it's out of their control, so they simply throw in the towel and don't try. This confuses the over 35's.

Take the environment as an example. Kids and young adults say they are worried about the environment being wrecked for their generation, but do they turn off the lights after leaving a room? Do they boycott eco unfriendly businesses? Do they protest? Do they bother to vote? Sadly, much of the time, the answer is no, but good news, voter registration is increasing. Interest is growing.

Both Brexit and Trump will have a massive impact on the young, yet the universities remain pretty much mute. The young adult vote could easily have swung the results of the Brexit referendum. Did the university students mobilise and protest and drive students to vote? No. Did they tell their parents and grandparents how they felt and argue their case – and lay a guilt trip on them? Did they even attend the marches after the referendum or organise simultaneous ones on their campuses? No. I attended a couple of the anti-Brexit protests in central London. There were millions of protestors – and almost all of them were over the age of thirty-five!

Apathy is sad to witness. The Vietnam War and apartheid would never have ended had the university students not mobilised. There were non-stop protests and boycotts, and universities were forced not to invest in, nor deal with companies involved with South Africa. The same could and should have been the result for Brexit and Trump. It still can be. As for the environment, university protests and young people's votes can make all the difference. To the young who are reading this, you are big in number and if you continue to get organised people will listen to you. And it is happening. More than 300 organizations, including many youth ones, are planning major climate strikes in the runup to the US 2020 elections.[59]

In Edinburgh the council decided to give students a day off once a year to strike in protest. As soon as I heard this I choked. A day off is not a strike. It's a day off, it quiets students' voices and trivialises what they're saying. But, thankfully the students knew what a strike was and didn't agree.[60] For them, it's when Greta skips school for two weeks to spend the time in front of the Swedish parliament handing out flyers. This is what gets a protest noticed. Not a day off school.

Today's young adults are truly wonderful people – they care more for others than any previous generation. They are more accepting of different types of people and don't like to see injustices. I admire their social awareness. IMHO, the young are the fairest and most noble generation that the world has ever seen – but to the young I say, I wish you would get off your asses to protest and vote! Let your beautiful voices be heard.

To the kids, university students and young adults of today: you *can* make a difference. You *must* make a difference. The world is counting on you and literally needs you to save it – environmentally and socially. You value people and the environment and you need to protect your values. You have the right values; you have heart and now it's time for you to persuade the old stick-in-the-muds to value these as well. We need each and every one of you. Together you are powerful. Your vote does count! Your presence at a democratic protest does count! The world needs you desperately. Find your voice and convince the older generation to step into line. You most certainly can change things, and what's more, you'll feel great doing it!

The Nordic countries

A brief mention of the Scandinavian countries is required here. Although Norway, Denmark, Sweden and Finland all have different economies, they have much in common and society is felt to be responsible for the individual. They often come tops in happiness, safety, education and welfare. The rest of the world is envious, but we are not rushing to copy their model. Why? Because they accomplish this with high taxation and that has become a 'no, no' phrase in many countries, although that view is beginning to change among today's young, including in the US.

In a way though, it's all a bit of a moot point: while these models are to be applauded, they too will need to change. The reason is simple – shrinking tax bases and ageing populations. Forty years from now they won't have the tax base to support their current infrastructures. They'll need to change as well. They're in the same shrinking/ageing population boat as everyone else. And of course, AI and the environment are vital concerns that they too will need to address.

At the heart of everything is wealth inequality. Whether it's health, education or the environment, they are all impacted by finance. Money.

Wealth Inequality

The three richest people in the US own more than the bottom 50% of the country.[61] Think about it. Three people are 'worth' more than 160 million people. This needs addressing immediately.

All the forces that have led us, over the last one hundred years, to our current situation - where economic prosperity and rampant consumerism co-exist with homelessness, begging and food banks - have also led to the growth of wealth, and income inequality as well as political turmoil. Not just inequality between the middle classes and the poor, but between the super-rich and the middle classes. It's a ticking time bomb and if we don't address it, it will blow up, as it has before. The problem is not the rich, it's the super-rich and if the super-rich keep on saying, 'let them eat cake', social unrest is sure to follow.

The Super-rich

The world's billionaires are growing $2.5 billion richer every day, while the poorest half of the global population is seeing its net worth dwindle every day. There are now 2,208 billionaires.

The combined fortunes of the world's 26 richest individuals reached $1.4 trillion last year – the same amount as the total wealth of the 3.8 billion poorest people.[62] In 2019, the world's richest 500 people increased their wealth by 25% or $1.2 trillion.[63]

In the US since 1989, the top 1% of rich people increased their wealth by $21 trillion to $29.6 trillion while the bottom 50% dropped $900 billion to -$200 billion.[64] And let's not forget the $30 trillion stashed in offshore tax havens.[65]

This is a problem that needs addressing now – otherwise we're in for a crash.

Total Wealth of Top 1% and Bottom 50% (1989-2018)

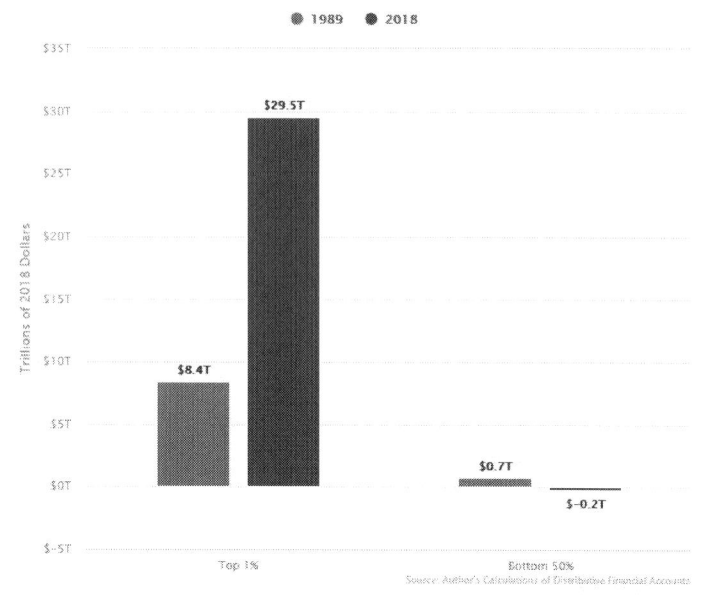

● 1989   ● 2018

- Top 1%: $8.4T (1989), $29.5T (2018)
- Bottom 50%: $0.7T (1989), $-0.2T (2018)

Source: Author's Calculations of Distributive Financial Accounts

2018 [66]

Distribution of Family Wealth (2016)

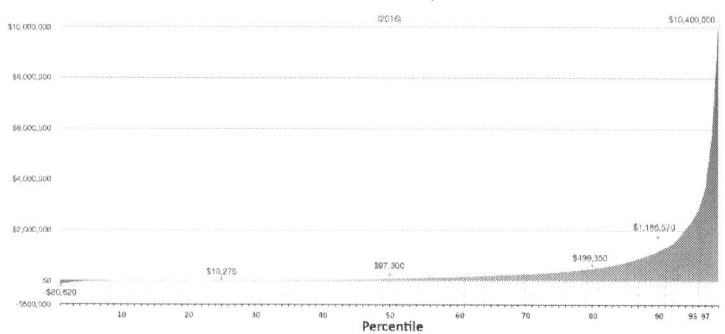

- 50th percentile: -$20,620 (shown at low end)
- 10th: $10,275
- 50: $97,300
- ~80: $499,350
- ~90: $1,186,570
- 97: $10,400,000

2018 [67]

45

There's not a bell curve in sight. And don't be misled by the '10% who own over 50% of the world's assets' story. It's extremely misleading. If someone is earning $150,000 a year, they're in that bracket. They're not rich. Upper middle class sure, but not super-rich by any stretch. Nor are those that are earning millions of dollars a year the problem. These stats are misleading. These people aren't the problem, either. They're wealthy and rich, but not super-rich.

%	Wealth $trn	Household Income
1	$33	$330,000 Rich
90-99	$41	$114,000 Upper Middle Class
50-90	$35	$39,000 Middle Class
50	$6	Lower Class

And the gap between the super-rich and the top 20% is very wide. The super-rich are the ones we need to tax. They are the problem.

Even the Gap Between the Top 1% and the Top 20% is Huge
U.S. before-tax income by income group, 2015

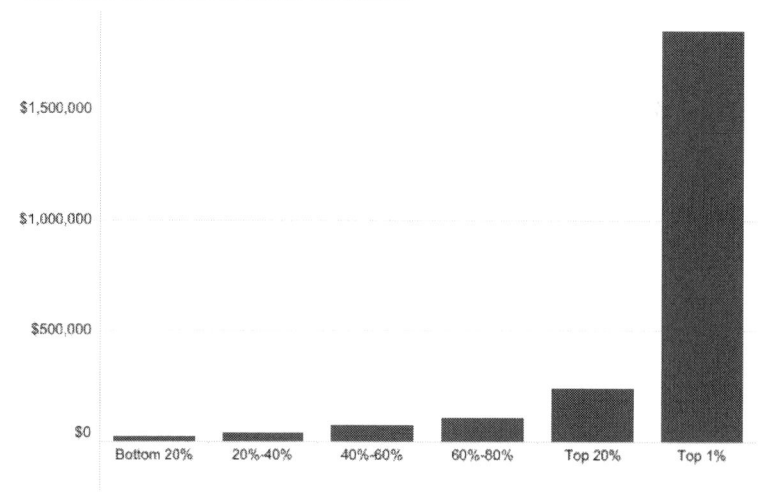

Source: Congressional Budget Office

Let's take a look at what the .1% have. They are the ones we need to focus on – and tax.

Richest 0.1% Take in 188 Times As Much as Bottom 90%
U.S. average income, 2017

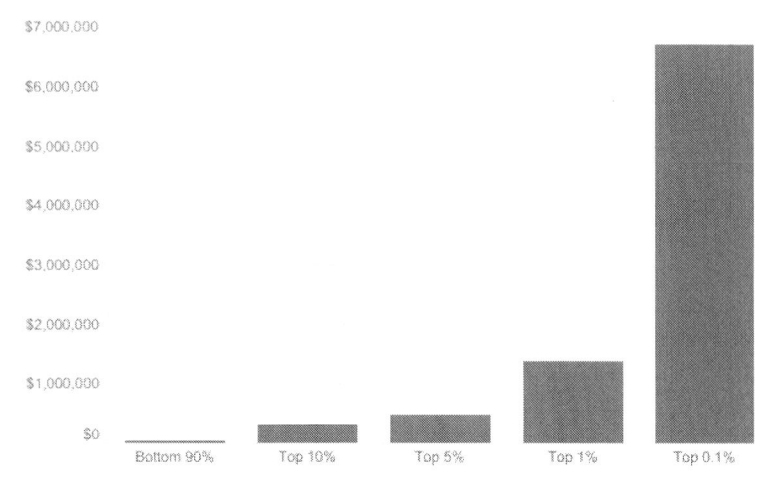

Source: Emmanuel Saez, UC Berkeley

The super-rich of the 2020's have all the wealth, as they did in the 1920's, and we know how that played out. We had ourselves back on course after the Second World War, but we began to mess things up again in the late 1970's.

The following graph clearly reflects the good times, between the end of the Second World War and the 1980's, when income distribution was more equitable. Since then, trickledown economics and neoliberalism have allowed the super-rich and the financiers to manipulate money. The present financial inequality we see is the result.

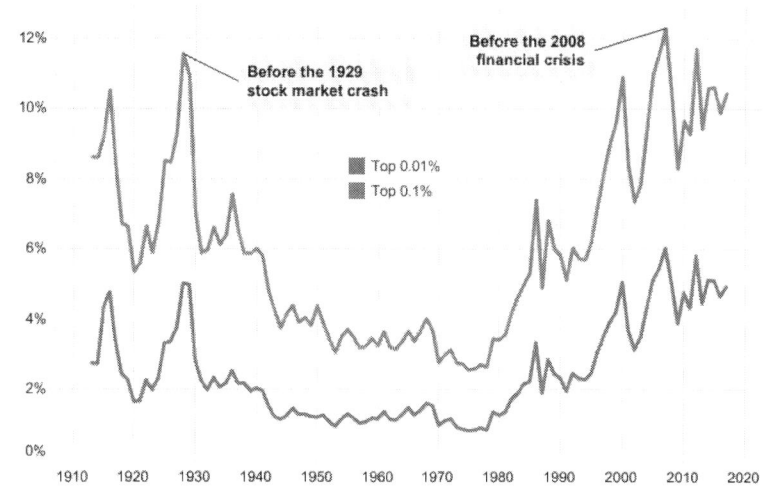

Income Concentration Has Returned to Gilded Age Levels
Share of total U.S. income going to the top 0.1% and top 0.01%, 1913-2017

Source: Emmanuel Saez, UC Berkeley

These lines correspond with the reduction in the top rate of income tax from the 1970's on. The lower the tax rate, the wider the inequality.

And this inequality continues to grow. Something's gotta' give. Interestingly enough, some of the people at the very top of the super-rich pyramid agree that things have to change, including a group called Patriotic Millionaires,[68] which is chaired by Morris Pearl, a former Managing Director of Blackrock, the world's largest Hedge Fund, and billionaire Nick Hanauer who says the rich have to stop this inequality or there will be pitchforks at their mansion gates.[69]

The 1920's looks suspiciously like the 2020's with the super-rich getting most of the US national income. And we know what happens when the rich have too much. Markets crash and the rest of us, the 99%, are left to pick up the tab for their gambling.

It's no better on a global scale - a few super-rich own most of the world.

The $5 Million-plus Club Holds Most of the World Millionaire Wealth
Share of world millionaire wealth by wealth group, 2017

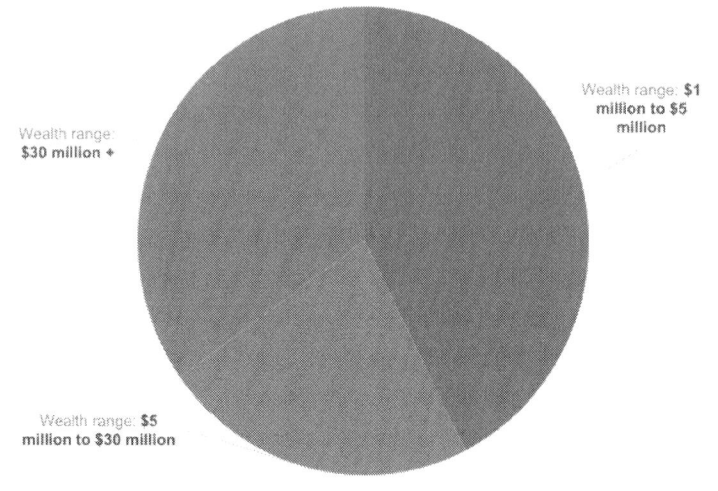

Wealth range: $1 million to $5 million

Wealth range: $30 million +

Wealth range: $5 million to $30 million

Source: Capgemini and RBC Wealth Management, World Health Report, 2018

Of course, it's not just the US and the UK that have seen a spike in super wealthy people – it's a global issue. The communists are no better. Russia had a bit of a spike as they let the oligarchs out after the fall of the USSR, and China has done a cracker of a job steadily creating 'capitalist pigs' since it joined the global markets.

Inequality is Rising or Staying High Nearly Everywhere
Top 10% incoe shares across the world, 1980-2016

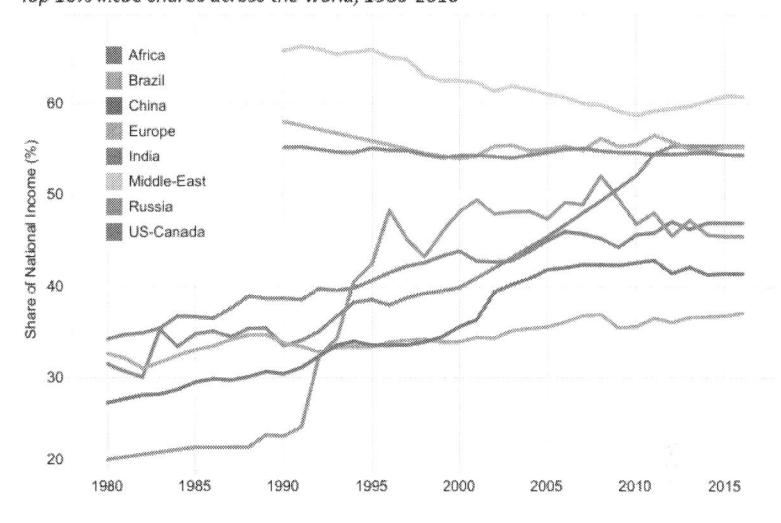

Source: World Inequality Lab, World Inequality Report, 2018

And the super-rich are no more deserving of riches than anyone else, although they believe they are. Much of their good fortune is simply due to luck.

Luck

Warren Buffett is a great believer in luck, and he believes it begins at birth. He calls it 'the ovarian lottery'. He recognises his luck to be born in the US and even admits he would not have been as 'lucky' had he been born a woman, rather than a man.[70]

What he's talking about is being born into the right environment, one that gave him and others the freedom to prosper, an environment with a governmental system of taxation that allowed people and businesses to prosper. While government may not be perfect, far from it, we need to stop looking at taxes as bad. Taxes are what allow our governments to provide the infrastructure we need to live well and safely. The lottery infrastructure that Buffett refers to is being dismantled and as he and many others, such as the group Patriotic Millionaires, advocate, the rich need to pay more tax. As Buffet has famously said, it's wrong that he pays a lower rate of tax than his secretary.[71] The problem is the super-rich not paying their fair share of tax. The beneficiaries of low taxes and 'tax breaks' are the rich. The losers are everyone else – the 80% of the population earning less than $60,000 a year.

Going a step further, we can now discount the old adage, 'the harder I work, the luckier I get'. The verdict is in. It's simply not true. Some of the hardest workers earn the least and billionaires do not work billions of time harder than everyone else. For sure, the wealthiest are definitely *not* the smartest, nor those with the most skills. Luck is the differentiator. Random luck. It's a phenomenon that has now been proven scientifically by the folks at the University of Catania in Italy.[72] They came up with a computer model to look at the 80/20 rule, otherwise known as the Pareto Principal, in which 20% have most of the wealth, based on human talent and how opportunities are exploited. This model allowed them to study chance. They charted the average working life of some people over forty years and entered this into the model. To their surprise, they found it mirrored the 80/20 rule showing that 20% randomly got lucky and had 80% of the wealth, and there was no correlation whatsoever with talent, including hard work or IQ etc. In fact, typically, the wealthiest were not the most talented.

That is not to say that wealthy people don't work hard. Many do and some are very, very smart and they do deserve their successes. However, there's no denying, luck played a role in their success and there's nothing wrong with admitting it. I'd be proud to be that lucky. In fact, most people are envious of that kind of luck. Often though, the wealthy want to believe it's all down to them, no luck involved. I really don't understand why. There's nothing wrong with luck, especially when coupled with hard work. It's a winning combination.

Financial inequality has got out of hand and needs to be reined in.

That lucky environment is not so lucky for most people anymore.

The Money Tree – How Things Work

Money

In order to have an idea of how everything works we need an understanding of money and how the global financial system works. It is core. It's truly what makes the world go round today. Money and finance are at the root of everything and together have been a prime motivator through the ages.

Why are the super-rich so rich? Money has existed in one guise or another from when we began to exchange things. It's been represented by silver, gold, shells, $, £, € and is certainly a lot easier to carry around than various parts of a cow to exchange for shoes, wheat and milk. That's why we have money.

Money is supposed to be simply a common means of exchange. But, it's far more and I will attempt to explain it to those who aren't very familiar with its nuances since it is fundamental to where we are and what comes next.

We must spend time on money because we can't fix today's issues if we don't understand a bit about it. Let's start with actual money, aka currency.

Currency

Money is a means of exchange. Money is only worth something if you can exchange it for something 'real'. That's why for most of current history, say the last 8,000 years or so, precious items like gold, silver, and even salt have represented 'money'. These items were rare, so people found comfort knowing that others would accept them as 'currency' for exchange. As monarchies and leaders carved out 'safe' areas, some of them began to make coins to represent money. These currencies were 'backed' by the 'assets' of gold, silver and other precious items that the dictator, king, or whoever supposedly held. The value of the coins being 'minted' fluctuated based on trust. The stronger the empire's influence, the further outside their borders the currency was accepted and 'trusted'.

If people felt that an empire had minted more money than the regime backing it had in assets, they would sell the currency. Increased selling would make it worth less. Lots of selling would devalue the currency, so it wouldn't be worth as much or maybe wouldn't even be accepted at all.

A natural trend in harmonisation made gold the defacto 'asset' behind currencies. Regardless of where they were from, people accepted the precious item. Remember all those empires exploring the world searching for gold? We have seen many gold rushes and it was, and remains, the most liquid asset globally. Everyone will accept it.

Currencies were minted and backed by national treasuries that stored gold. This made it easier for people to trust the currency, as historically, gold was the most easily accepted precious item. That's why during the Gulf wars and the 2008 crash, the price of gold rocketed. It was felt to be a safe asset. That's why even today people hide gold under their beds and literally wear their wealth in jewellery. Gold is real. Gold is tangible. We trust gold. That's also why after the US assassinated the Iranian General Soleimani on Jan 3, 2020, gold jumped to highs of $1,600 per ounce.

Gold has been used as currency for roughly 5,000 years. Paper money only first began to have an impact in the 1700's. For much of that time governments stored gold to 'back' their currencies. This created The Gold Standard and it morphed through the years. Its high point was between the early 1800's and the late 1960's. In 1944 most countries signed up to the Bretton Woods Agreement, whereby all currencies were linked to the US dollar and the US dollar was linked to gold. This briefly put the US dollar as the world's reserve currency. This, and the gold standard, ended in the late 1960's and governments began to print money as they saw fit. Enter the era of 'fiat money' that we are in now.

Fiat money: *fiat money is a currency without intrinsic value that has been established as money, often by government regulation. Fiat money does not have use value, and has value only because a government maintains its value, or because parties engaging in exchange agree on its value.*[73] *Fiat money is government-issued currency that is not backed by a physical commodity, such as gold or silver, but rather by the government that issued it.*[74]

In other words, todays' currencies are created by governments putting their fingers in the air and deciding how much money to print. These currencies have no basis in reality.

Currencies no longer needed to be backed by gold and the US dollar became the defacto world currency. Governments could and do print as much money as they want – trillions since the crash of 2008. But how can they do this? Where is the value the paper represents? It's not like there were a hundred more cows created or twenty more chairs or iPhones produced, or that there was a stash of gold behind the printing. Where's the value behind the currency? There isn't any. It's a social construct that represents the good faith of the country to give you back... what exactly? Nothing? Nothing, but more paper that is also printed on demand.

Currencies fluctuate against each other depending on demand for that country's currency, which is impacted by things such as political uncertainty, war, Brexit, economic growth etc. One day it may take $1 to exchange for £1, while the next it could be $1 to exchange for £0.50. If you had $2 in the US and were buying a cup for £1 from the UK at an exchange rate of $1 to £1, you'd be able to buy two cups for $2. If the exchange rate moves to $1 equals £0.5, the price to buy the £1, is now $2 to you. The previously $1 cup would now cost you $2. You can only buy one now. The cup doubled in price because the £ doubled in value against the $.

$1 = £1
1 cup costs £1 ($1). You have $2 so you can buy 2 cups

$1 = £0.50 (50 pence)
1 cup costs £1 ($2). You have $2 so you can buy 1 cup

Same cup but double the price to you. Nothing to do with the cup's intrinsic value at all. Just the currency's 'value' as determined by 'investors' and 'speculators'. In other words, currencies are make-believe and have become their own 'value', not connected directly to an asset or output (service). The supply of currency is not dependent on actual economic output. It's just what the government decides to print.

As currencies are not tied to anything tangible, they're not real, which makes them rife for speculation. While 'investment bankers' may make money by speculating, both businesses and people are at their whim, sometimes benefitting, and sometimes hurting from their speculation.

Let's take two cup makers in two different countries. The exchange rate is $1 equals £1. Both cup makers pay the same amount for the things needed to make the cup and take as long to make the cup. They are equally efficient. They both sell their cups in their country, for $1 and £1. The extra cost of shipping means that both cup makers are focused on their local markets.

Now, what happens if the $ is devalued against the £? Say, to $1 equals £0.50 (50 pence) in this case? The price for making the cups in each country has remained the same, but the retail cost has changed abroad. The UK shopper, with £1, could buy one UK cup for £1 or they could buy two US cups for £1. Guess what the shopper will do?

Of course, the US cup maker grabs this opportunity and begins to sell more cups in the UK. Eventually, the UK cup maker must fire their one hundred staff and close the business and three hundred people – staff and their families – just lost their livelihood, through no fault of their own, just a change in a fiat (fictional) currency. Simplification I know, but I think you get the gist.

This is why countries sometimes devalue their currency. It helps their businesses as it makes their products (exports) cheaper globally and makes imports more expensive, which protects their home markets.

Another major thing related to currencies happened after the Second World War. A number of countries tied their national currencies to the US dollar and then most natural resources were priced in US dollars. They still are, and the US fights off any attempts to change this. It makes sense as they have an amazingly unfair global trading advantage. Let me explain. Remember the automotive revolution also included oil, and lots of other minerals. All were priced in US dollars. If the price of oil goes up or down, it goes up and down for everyone. Therefore, petrol stations, shipping companies and electricity suppliers etc. must all raise their prices globally.

But, what happens if you are a petrol station or power supplier based somewhere other than the US, the UK for instance, and the dollar strengthens against the pound? From $1 equals £1, to $1 equals £2, so the oil that cost you $1 (£1) before now costs you £2. You need to raise your prices and pass your costs on. The US petrol station and power supplier don't need to. They don't have the same exchange rate risk as other countries. It gives the US a massive trading advantage. Resources being pegged to the US dollar removes a huge element of uncertainty and risk for USD businesses.

Clearly, it's difficult not to agree that currencies are pretty bogus. They're arbitrarily unfair and the world would be a better place without multiple currencies.

Crypto currencies

Bitcoin et al

By now, most people have heard of cryptocurrencies, even if they don't understand what they are. On the one hand, they can appear confusing, but in reality, they are fairly straightforward; the premise behind them being that as currencies today are not real, why not make a decentralised digital currency? Make digital bits and bytes the 'gold'. It's just numbers after all. Let's use Bitcoin, the most famous one, as our example, as they are all pretty similar.

In a nutshell, just like the gold miners of the past, 'miners' today mine for Bitcoins ('bit' as in computer 'bits' and 'bytes'). While traditional gold miners used picks and shovels to mine for gold, today's miners use computers to create digital coins. Thing is, even worse than a currency being backed by gold, which is at least an asset, these digital currencies are total make-believe. They do not represent chairs, cows, iPhones, time, or even gold. Cryptocurrencies have absolutely no relationship to any value whatsoever.

A study in March 2019 said that most Bitcoin trades are fake. It seems 95% of the trading in these fictional currencies is, well... fiction.[75]

Libra - the new FB currency

Yes, Facebook is making its own currency. But it's not a cryptocurrency. It will be a currency representing a basket of currencies and its headquarters will be in that bastion of transparency, Switzerland. What can I say? If you're more comfortable with thirty corporations like Facebook, Uber, Spotify, Visa and Mastercard controlling the world's money supply for the benefit of their shareholders, then go for it. Good news though, this group appears to have started falling apart in late 2019.

As well as this, Facebook (or Google or Apple for that matter) are companies and could be gone tomorrow. Personally, I wouldn't touch Libra. The fundamental ingredient in a currency is trust. I do not trust companies with shareholders to run currencies. Do you?

Facebook wants to be our digital identity through Libra and its digital wallet Calibra – which it's spun off as a separate marketing company. So it can sell us stuff by harvesting and selling our personal data to companies like Cambridge Analytica? And that's only one company. There are plenty of others that Facebook sells our information to.

How can we trust a company that says it doesn't listen to our private chats through our phone, but clearly does?[76] Like many people, I noticed this a few years ago and have run tests. We would talk about an obscure product and then a few hours later, ads for that product appeared on Facebook.[77] We've tested this dozens of times with everything from mosquito nets in March to car scratch removers, car taillights and cat food. It's no coincidence. The ads appear for a short while, and then disappear. Try it.

In August 2019 Facebook admitted it also pays a team of people to listen to and transcribe your Messenger conversations.[78] They're listening and watching – Amazon just admitted *Alexa does* listen and store your private conversations,[79] and then there's Google's *Assistant* and Apple's *Siri*.

This joke kind of says it all:

> MY WIFE ASKED ME WHY I
> SPOKE SO SOFTLY IN THE
> HOUSE.
> I SAID I WAS AFRAID
> MARK ZUCKERBERG WAS
> LISTENING!
> SHE LAUGHED.
> I LAUGHED.
> ALEXA LAUGHED.
> SIRI LAUGHED.

It's an invasion of our privacy on an unprecedented scale. And when these companies get caught, the fines are a joke, even if they sound like a lot, they're not. Facebook has just been fined $5 billion by the Federal

Trade Commission (FTC) for the Cambridge Analytica stuff, the Trump and Brexit votes tampering outfit. It may sound like a big fine, but it's not. Facebook made $22bn in profit last year. Added to that, minutes after the announcement, Facebook's stock went up more than $5bn (making Zuckerberg even richer). He and the other shareholders were rewarded, not penalised, for breaking the law and abusing our trust by selling our privacy.[80] Lawyer, technologist and writer, Albert Fox Cahn who founded STOP, the Surveillance Technology Oversight's Project to protect our civil rights, lays out a compelling argument for jail time instead of fines for privacy abuse. As Cahn points out, fines are regarded as merely a cost of doing business. He uses price fixing as an example, where fines increased but price fixing continued. It didn't slow down until the first people started going to jail.[81] It doesn't even need to be a long sentence to be effective.

Global Currency

Don't get me wrong. I do believe that having one currency for the world could be good – call it digital if you want. The first thing though is that we would have to think about what it represents, i.e., who gets to print it and for what reason.

Imagine the entire world using the US dollar. Yeah, yeah, if you want to keep £ then it can be permanently fixed to the $. Exchange rate risk and speculation would be wiped out overnight. It would be a level playing field, globally. Great. But we certainly don't want the US deciding how many of them there are in total, and who gets them?

We almost had a global trading currency launched in 1944 at Bretton Woods. Developed by Keynes and promoted by the UK, it was called bancor.[82] Unfortunately, the US had other ideas and wanted the US dollar to be the global currency.

All fiat currencies have associated interest rates. Interest is what people, governments and businesses pay to borrow or lend money. Interest is paid on debt and deposits. And that debt is now traded in the financial markets. Debt and interest rates are central to the current financial inequality.

Interest

An understanding of debt and interest is necessary to get a handle on money, since money (having it, not having it, or getting more of it) plays such a huge role in human motivation and behaviour. Acquiring it in some form or other, has been our prime motivator throughout our history, so it's worth getting to grips with its complexities, even if it's not exactly as riveting as a thriller (although thrillers, books and films, have been made about it!)

At the core of debt is interest.

Warren Buffet loves compound interest. Others view interest as usurious. So, what is it? In a nutshell it's what person A pays person B to borrow money. That money could be used to create a new business, buy a car or house, or put food on the table. While the concept in itself is not bad, what can be bad is the interest rate. And the fundamental problem here is that those who can least afford the 'loan' pay the highest interest rates. To see this in action, let's look at the graph following.

Each person borrowed $10,000 and is paying $188.71 a month towards it. Both people are 'low risk'. One person borrowed at a 5% interest rate and the other person got a credit card and borrowed at a 30% interest rate, the rate on many credit cards – what's yours? Check it out! In 60 months the 5% loan is completely repaid. In 60 months the 30% loan is now $18,300.

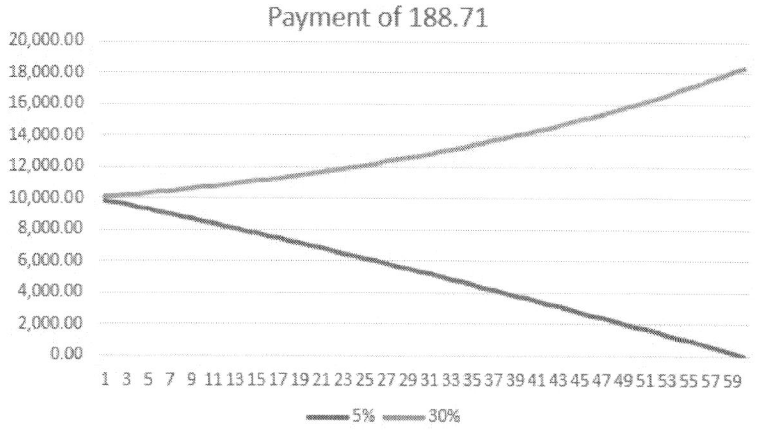
Payment of 188.71
20,000.00
18,000.00
16,000.00
14,000.00
12,000.00
10,000.00
8,000.00
6,000.00
4,000.00
2,000.00
0.00
1 3 5 7 9 11 13 15 17 19 21 23 25 27 29 31 33 35 37 39 41 43 45 47 49 51 53 55 57 59
5%
30%

The sad thing now is that the person with the credit card who is a good credit risk goes to the bank and says, 'I'd like to cancel my card and turn it into a loan.' The bank will often reply, 'No, you've already borrowed as much as our systems say you can.' Even though the person is willing to cancel the card, he or she is still stuck and going deeper in debt.

Now let's look at each person's payments based on repaying the loan in 5 years (60 months).

This is the person with a $10,000 loan. Following are the principal and interest payments they make each month. They pay $188 a month for five years and a total of $1,300 in interest. They are always paying down the loan – more of their monthly payment is going towards the principal (the amount they borrowed) than towards interest.

5% Amount Financed	10,000.00
Payment Every Month	188.71
Total of 60 Payments	11,322.74
Total Interest	1,322.74
All Payments and Fees	11,322.74

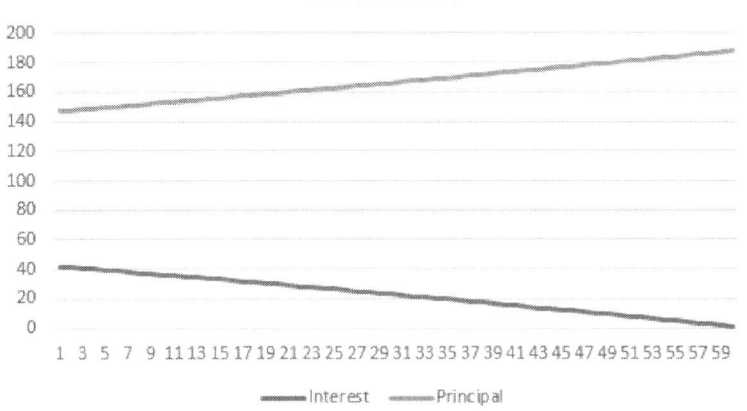

5% Interest

Now let's increase the payment for the person with the credit card so that they can repay the $10,000 loan they have on their card and see what happens. They need to pay $323 a month for 5 years and pay $9,400 in interest. It's not until month 33 that they are repaying more towards the principal (the amount they borrowed) than towards interest.

30%	Amount Financed	10,000.00
	Payment Every Month	323.53
	Total of 60 Payments	19,412.04
	Total Interest	9412.04
	All Payments and Fees	19,412.04

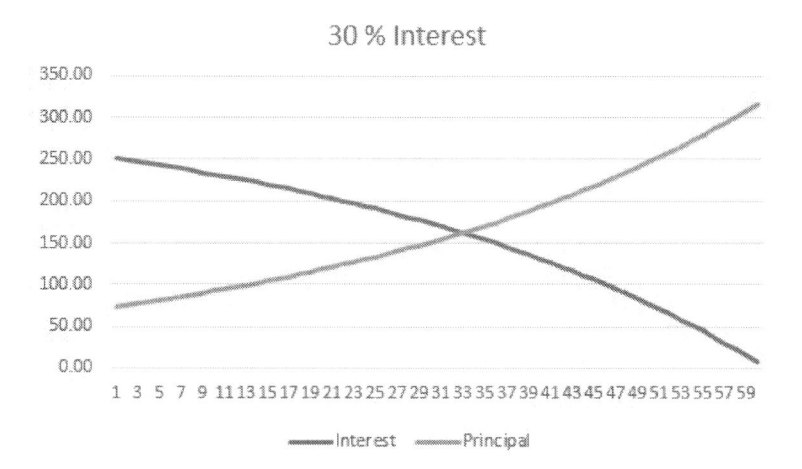

30 % Interest

It's scary. The person who can't convert the card to a loan is put into financial hardship. And you wonder why there are more defaults at 30% than 5%...?

The credit card companies are nothing more than loan sharks. This wasn't always the case and now in the US, Alexandria Ocasio-Cortez and Bernie Sanders are advocating bringing back the maximum interest on credit cards to 15%, which is what it used to be until deregulation in the late 70's and early 80's. [83]

Now imagine those people really struggling to pay their children's school meals, the ones who must take out payday loans. These are short term loans that people take at very high interest rates to survive from paycheck to paycheck. The industry calls them 'high risk' and at these interest rates it's easy to understand why. Anyone who needs to borrow at 400% interest is high risk, simply due to the interest rate.

Just so you can really get a handle on payday loans that have average rates of 400%, let's look at $1,000 for one year in a graph. On a $1,000 loan, borrowers pay over $3,000 in interest. It's only in the last two months, the point where the two lines cross, that they are paying more towards the principal (the money they borrowed) than interest. The interest is three times more than what they originally borrowed. They paid $4,000 for $1,000 worth of food. Who benefits? The loan sharks. Until the end of the 70's the US had a cap on interest rates at 15%. Now you can see why.

400% Amount Financed	1,000.00
Payment Every Month	344.24
Total of 60 Payments	4,130.85
Total Interest	3,130.85
All Payments and Fees	4,130.85

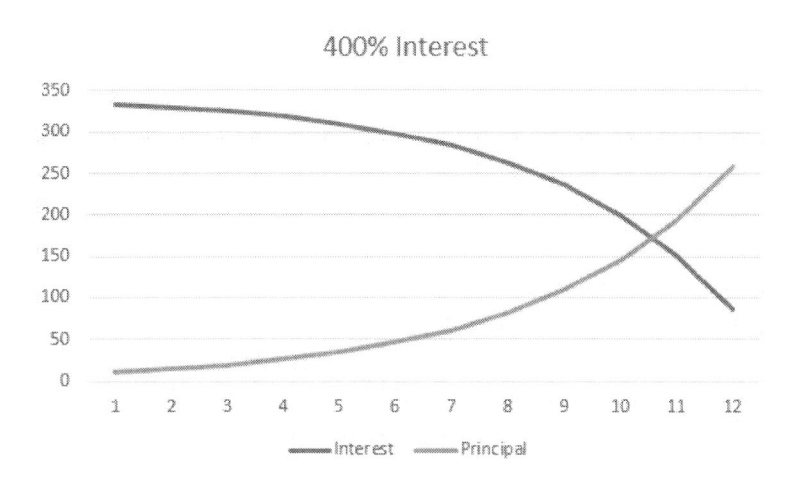

400% Interest

This is usurious and should be illegal. Imagine the current situation where people need to take out payday loans to get money to put food on the table and they are charged interest on the loan at 100's of percent. Not that credit cards charging 30% interest are much better, but that's an improvement from 100's of percent. Seems to me if everyone had similar interest rates, not only would it be fairer, but there would be fewer defaults. Lend what someone can afford or don't lend at all. If someone can 'afford' a loan at 400%, they can certainly afford one at 5%. And funnily enough, they would be less likely to need a loan to put food on the table, as their whole paycheck wouldn't be going on interest payments.

Out of curiosity, let's see what the 'good' credit risk person pays to borrow $1,000 at the 5% annual interest for a year. $27 in interest, plus monthly payments of $85 vs. $344 a month payment, and $3,000 in interest for the 'high risk' person - and you wonder why the 'high risk' person, paying 400% interest, defaults and then gets categorised as a bad credit risk. Yeah, right. This is simply wrong. No two ways about it.

5% Amount Financed	1,000.00
Payment Every Month	85.61
Total of 60 Payments	1,027.29
Total Interest	27.29
All Payments and Fees	1,027.29

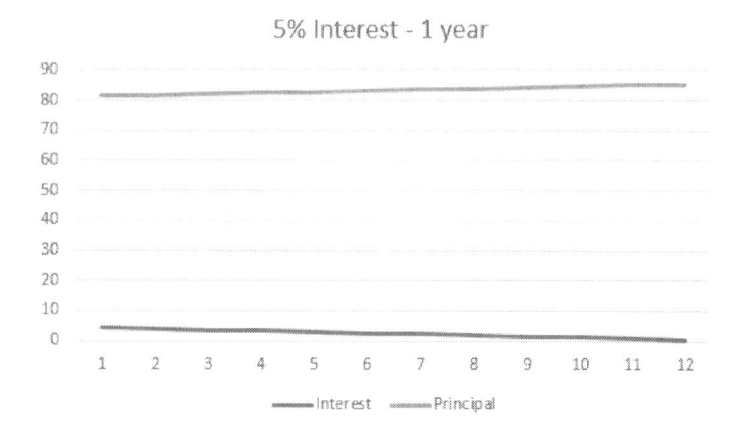

5% Interest - 1 year

Banking

Now that we know more about money and interest, we need to look at banking.

This is a top-level explanation of banking. Some people will already know this. Some will know some of this. For others, a lot of this will be new. As finance is at the centre of how the super-rich have and keep power, we need to understand it better. It also directly impacts all the other issues, such as the environment, health and social.

While banking is very important, there are those who earn tremendous amounts of money in 'finance' by playing with numbers and manipulating cash flows – usually debt (loans). They are the financiers and they are *not* Makers; they *are* Takers.[84]

There are two main types of banking that the financiers work in – Retail and Investment. At various times throughout history these two types of banking have been separate or combined. Each time they've been combined it's been a disaster.

Retail Banking

Retail banking is fairly easy to understand. People and businesses deposit money in banks. The bank pays interest to the depositor at say 4%. People and businesses need to borrow money for expensive items, such as mortgages or to fund business growth, as these require large amounts. The bank lends out our money to these people and businesses at 6%. The bank makes 2% (6% - 4%), which covers their running costs and creates profit. All of which is very useful to society.

A quick mention about Credit Unions and Building Societies – they are both banks but use their profits to provide better services and higher interest rates to 'members' and to reduce member borrowing fees. They may pay depositors say 4.5% interest, instead of 4%, and lend money at 5.50%, instead of 6%.

Retail banks traditionally don't like volatility and avoid it. They have a very straight forward and socially valuable business model – as long as rates are not usurious.

Investment Banking

Investment banks used to be called merchant banks and they are very different to retail banks. Merchant banks were there to facilitate trade and business growth. They had relationships with other banks around the world to enable businesses to pay safely for goods and services. They charged businesses a fee for using these services. They also helped people and companies raise finance for new ventures. They did this by using their own cash or by creating syndicates and investment partnerships, which in time evolved into shareholders. Basically, wealthy people and businesses with excess cash invested in the merchant banks, which gave the banks the money to conduct their business. These banks facilitated trade in goods and services and have played a very important role throughout our history starting in the Middle Ages – and these services continue to be required today.

In the past, once people had invested in syndicates, there was very little 'liquidity' (the ability to buy or sell something easily). If, for some reason, an investor needed some of their investment cash back, they would have to try and find someone to buy their stake. The bank would often help find a buyer. This could be difficult to do though, and of course, deciding a price was not easy because a forced seller would be in a weaker negotiating position.

As more businesses wanted to raise finance, by selling shares and debt, and as wealthy people wanted to be able to buy and sell their shares (liquidity), a trading exchange was needed; a neutral place where merchant banks could buy and sell shares for their clients, a place where merchant banks could offer (list) new shares in companies and invite other merchant banks to have their clients buy them. In 1602 the Dutch East India Company was the first to list shares on the Amsterdam Stock Exchange. It was also the first company to issue stocks and bonds. And so, we entered a new financial era.

Merchant banks began to turn into investment banks – a way to invest in assets. Companies and governments would raise finance, and wealthy people would buy and sell shares and debt through them. These banks would bring new companies to market (list them on the stock exchange), by finding investors who wished to invest by buying those shares.

The first big crash was not too far behind, you might have heard of it, the Tulip rush of the 1630's. Tulips were new to Europe and became very fashionable. Everyone wanted tulips and the bulbs to grow them. Speculation was rife and at one point, one tulip bulb was worth more than an entire family estate. Then, they plummeted, and a tulip became worth the price of a cabbage. Their prices may have changed, but the underlying asset, the real thing, (the tulip, the family estate and the cabbage) remained the same.

Financial bubbles are always around assets, not goods and services. The tulip bulb might have been more expensive than an entire family estate, but it was not really more valuable, not really 'worth' more. Yet, in money terms, it was. And in business parlance, something is only worth as much as someone is willing to pay for it, hence regular asset bubbles and crashes. Hence the financial crash of 2008.

As you can see, investment banking is a whole other beast to retail banking. Investment banks love volatility. They want prices to change and markets to move up or down so that they can make money as intermediaries. They don't care which way the market goes. As it is stands now, it's mostly a giant money casino, one where investment bankers bet other people's money and keep the winnings when they win. But, when they lose, they lose nothing themselves as it's not their money they're risking. From a gambler's perspective, you couldn't have a better situation. It's all upside.

These may all be simplifications and generalisations, but this is why the 2008 crash happened. The taxpayers footed the gambling debt, while the investment bankers kept their beach houses.

Shares

Shares are also called equity. They are investments in a business in exchange for part ownership of that business. You own a share of the business. When the company makes a profit, you share in that profit. The company distributes a percentage of these profits to its owners, the shareholders. This is called a dividend. Some profit may be held back for future investment in the business.

One of the ways people decide and compare which share to buy or sell is based on P/E (Price to Earnings Ratio). Share price divided by earnings.

Traditionally, people who liked a company bought its shares. This is called going 'long'. They either liked its dividends or growth prospects, and expected the share value and profits to increase, so they bought the share for the long term.

As a straightforward example, you might buy 100 shares in a company that has 1,000 shares. You pay $1 for each share, so the total investment you make is $100. You own 10% of that business.

If the company makes $100 a year in profit (the money left over after all company running expenses have been paid), then it can share the profit amongst its owners. In other words, pay a dividend to its shareholders. $100 split between 1,000 shares is $0.10 per share. As you have 100 shares, it means you will receive $10, which is a pretty good 10% annual return. See column A.

		A	B	C
Investment	$100			
Price per share	$1.00			
Number of shares bought	100			
Total number of company shares	1,000			
Company value	$1,000			
Company profit		$100.00	$200.00	$50.00
Profit per share		$0.10	$0.20	$0.05
Profit from investment		$10.00	$20.00	$5.00
% Return		10.00%	20.00%	5.00%
Average Market Return 10%				
New Company Value		$1,000	$2,000	$500
New Share Price		$1.00	$2.00	$0.50
Share Sale Profit		$0	$100	-$50
% Profit		0%	100%	-50%

The price of the shares may go up or down. If the company is growing and making more profits, then you also hope the share price will rise to reflect this. Using the same example, say in year two, the company makes a $200 profit - that's $0.2 per share. You'll receive a dividend of $20, a 20% return. You're laughing and very happy. That's column B.

If you want to sell those shares, and if everyone else is happy with earning a 10% return and that's what other investments are paying, you'd be a fool to sell your share at the price you paid. The share price will need adjusting. In order for the return to be 10% like other investments, the share price would need to go up to $2 a share. $2 receiving $0.2 return is a 10% return.

So, you can sell your shares for $200 and give up the 20% annual return next year for a 100% increase in your original investment. You've doubled your money. Well done. Now you need to find the next company to invest in that is paying 10% and may go up to 20%.

Of course, this works in reverse as well. If the company were to make $50, then the return would be less, $0.05 per share, which is a 5% return. That's column C. If others are paying 10% and you wanted to sell your shares, you'd have to sell them at $0.5 a share. You'd only get $50 for your shares - a loss of 50%.

Liquidity

Liquidity is being able to easily buy or sell something. Just being listed on stock exchanges does not guarantee liquidity. To have liquidity you need the same number of buyers and sellers. If you want to buy a share, someone must be willing to sell it and the same in reverse. There are only ever a finite number of shares after all. This is what stock markets do. They show the prices people are willing to buy and sell shares at. If no one wants to buy a share, the price goes down, which increases the yield potential from the dividend to attract buyers. If everyone wants the share, the price goes up, as they're investing in the expected growth in share price and dividends that will result from profits generated in the future. In today's markets, prices can literally change millisecond-by-millisecond, especially in a fast-moving market.

To create what's called 'a market' in a company's shares, an investment bank offers to always buy and sell a company's shares, to 'make a market' for them. When a new company is listed, one or more investment banks will agree to make a market in those shares. They become the central point for those shares and know who is buying and selling and facilitate trading in those shares. These market makers get paid a fee for doing so.

Sometimes, someone may want to buy some shares, while there is no one who wants to sell any, or vice versa. So, the investment banks, these 'market makers', are allowed to sell the shares to Person A, even though the bank does not own any of these shares. The bank goes '*short*'. Then, usually, as quickly as possible, the bank finds someone who has shares that they want to sell to the bank, and the bank '*covers'* their position. The longer the market maker waits to buy these shares, the more risk the investment bank is exposed to, as the share price could change up or down. If it goes up, the bank loses money. If it goes down, they are OK.

This mechanism has generally kept the markets fairly stable, otherwise the price might rise really high to attract a seller, or vice versa, drop really low to attract a buyer – like at the end of the day.

There are strict rules about how long these '*positions*' can be kept open and how they are reported. The intent is to create market stability and to manage risk; not speculate. This is achieved by having a neutral middleman who always makes a market and maintains liquidity. Market making is a very important and crucial service.

Bonds

Bonds are debt.

Bonds have a fixed beginning and usually a fixed end date (the maturity date). They are loans and similar to an interest-only loan, whereby the 'principal' (the amount borrowed) is usually paid back at the end of the loan, and loan payments, during the loan term, are interest-only.

There are a few main types of bonds – government, corporate and mortgage. Mortgages are closer to regular bank loans in that they usually have principal and interest repaid during the term of the loan. They can also be repaid early and are secured ('collateralised') by the underlying property.

The difference between bonds and loans is that with bonds, the principal (the amount borrowed), is usually paid off in a lump sum at the end on the bond's maturity date. Furthermore, interest payments, made by a company on those bonds, are usually tax deductible, which can encourage companies to take on debt. Today, company debt is a cost before profits are worked out. In other words, debt lowers a company's tax bill. It's tax efficient to borrow money.

At the basic level, bonds work the same, and are based around interest rates. People invest in them as the investment is relatively safe and they may receive regular guaranteed income payments. This is ideal for many investment types, such as pension funds that must pay pensioners every month.

Unlike shareholders, bondholders don't own a company, but they have a stake in it through a different mechanism – the pecking order. If a company is to be closed, the bondholders are paid back their loans before anything left over is shared with the shareholders. In other words, bondholders come before shareholders in all pay-out situations.

Because of these things, bonds are considered a safer investment and more reliable income stream than shares.

Government bonds are pretty straightforward: the government borrows $100 for 10 years at a 10% interest rate. An investor will lend the government $100 today, receive $10 a year in interest, and be repaid the $100 when the ten years are up, as in Column A following. For 10 years the investor knows what their income will be. This is one of the reasons pension funds like bonds, and higher interest rates. They offer stable income streams to pay out to their pension holders – the higher the better for pension funds and pensioners.

So, what happens if interest rates change? Say they go to 20%, like in Column B. If you want to sell your bonds, no one is going to give you $100 for your bonds, as the return is only 10%. You need to drop the price of the bond until you reach a matching 20% return. In other words, you need to sell the bonds for $50 – a loss of 50% of your principal. Conversely, if interest rates drop to 5%, as in Column C, the bonds would be worth $200 for the same return, and you would have doubled your investment. As a friend once explained to me, think of bonds as airplanes, one wing is interest rates and the other wing is bond prices. When interest rates go up, bond prices go down. When interest rates go down, bond prices go up. Simples.

		A	B	C
Investment	$100			
Price per bond	$1.00			
Number of bonds bought	100			
Interest Rates		10.00%	20.00%	5.00%
New Bond Price		$1.00	$0.50	$2.00
Bond Sale Profit		$0	-$50	$100
% Profit		0%	-50%	100%

Mortgage backed securities (bonds) are primarily an American invention as most mortgages in the US have fixed interest rates and terms, which means that interest rates on traditional mortgages don't change. Thus, the interest rate is locked, often for twenty or thirty years.

When interest rates go down, Americans 'refinance' their mortgages at the lower interest rates. Wouldn't you? And when interest rates go up, they of course stay with their existing mortgage.

These mortgages are packaged into pools of 'similar' mortgages (credit risk and interest rate are two packaging factors) and sold to investors. They're popular as they usually provide a fairly stable and reliable cashflow for investors.

The subprime crash of 2008 was based around some of these mortgage-based bonds that were paying above average incomes. In reality these turned out to be high-risk mortgages (hence the higher returns), so customers began defaulting and stopped making their mortgage payments. Then, there was an avalanche of non-payments and house repossessions.

So, who were the investors in these shares and bonds? They were - and still are - pension funds, mutual funds, company investments, hedge funds, investment banks and individuals.

The bond market is larger than the equity (share) market. In the US, the bond market ($40 trillion) is roughly twice the size of the stock market ($20 trillion) and trading volumes are also much higher.

Derivatives

Derivatives are derived (based upon) financial instruments – shares, bonds, commodities and currencies. They used to be fairly straightforward and there were two primary types, futures and options. Initially, they were not overly complicated.

You may remember some crazy commodity price hikes in 2007 and 2008, everything from bread to petrol. Churches were having lead roofs stolen and people were stealing copper cabling. Most of this was due to commodities speculation. Lots of cash, low interest rates and investment banks being able to own commodities, meant that financial speculation by the financiers was driving prices up; there was plenty of supply, while demand was actually down. Large institutional investors were betting $13 billion in the commodities market in 2003. That rose to $260 billion in 2008. And twenty-five major commodities rose by 183% during that time.[85]

And then governments began to print fictional money in 2008, which they used to purchase bonds. This injected a lot of cash into the financial ecosystem and was/is called 'quantitative easing'. It was a response to the 2008 crash designed to avert an economic meltdown. What actually happened is that a few more trillion was made available to investors, to gamble and purchase assets with. It's only the end of quantitative easing that has finally begun to reverse the commodity and asset price hikes, as there's now less free money in the system.

Venture Capital

Venture capital plays a very important role for entrepreneurs and the investment ecosystem as a whole. Without it, most of today's companies wouldn't exist. Venture capitalists invest in companies they believe in – they go '*long*'. In a traditional route to business growth, typically an entrepreneur uses personal funds (and credit cards) and brings in friends and family as the first investors. Then, when the money needs become too large, the venture capitalists show up. They take risk and invest when the 'market' isn't ready, and when the investment required is more than friends and family can provide.

Generally speaking, venture capitalists serve a very important purpose by supplying funds, and often guidance and contacts, to companies as they grow. The more astute venture capitalists are those that have built businesses themselves or are visionaries who look to, and bet on, the future. They understand and have vision. They understand the risks. Who are venture capitalists? Some started their own businesses that had nothing to with venture capital and became venture capitalists after making their money; others built their own venture capital businesses, while others again, are bean counters.

Investing in early growth is about seeing the vision and taking risks. No bones about it, we need venture capitalists. They know what founders are going through and lend a hand. They are to be applauded. This is another good part of investment banking, as they help to create new businesses that benefit us all.

Sure, there are the bad apples. There are plain old accountants who, because they have their hands on the money tap, over-estimate their importance. There are these too: the pencil pushers and spreadsheet brigade. They control the money after all and hold the purse strings of other people's money – it can go to their heads.

Being an ex-banker and entrepreneur, I've had experience with both.

Private Equity (PEG)

Not to be confused with venture capital, private equity is a very different story. This is all about finance and working the numbers, the debt.

Simply stated, someone or a group of people, or a fund, buy a company lock, stock and barrel. They buy all the shares and then supposedly manage the company. They do this through financial engineering. Accountancy stuff. Not building the business.[86] The company being bought could be in distress but have assets such as property. It will likely have lots of value in it that can be realised. In most situations it has assets that can be sold or borrowed against. Private equity usually doesn't take any real risk, yet many like to call themselves 'turn around specialists' for turning businesses around – usually at the cost of existing shareholders, bond holders and staff.[87] The reality is the PEGs (Private Equity Groups) don't create value; they extract value from existing businesses. They extract so much value for themselves that they weaken, or even wreck, the business, sometimes lethally.

PEGs want to make money. They find a company that has good cashflow (revenues), possibly some fixed assets like real estate and little debt – the kind of company that would be a good, safe and stable investment – and they buy it. So far, this sounds sensible and like normal investing and everything makes sense.

The thing is, they don't actually invest much of their own money, they just want to make money.[88] Nothing wrong with that per se, but how does the PEG buy it then? A private equity group will buy a healthy company that has little debt and is generating good revenue without using its own money. Instead of using their money, the PEG borrows it – actually the company borrows it. This is how it works.

A company with little debt and good revenue can borrow a lot of money. The PEG approaches the banks and says it's going to buy a company. The company makes a profit of 100 million a year and has no debt, and they would like to borrow 1 billion and use the 100 million in profit every year to pay the banks loan payments of 80 million due every year.

The bank says OK, so the PEG buys all the shares off the company's shareholders for 700 million. They use the 1 billion from the banks to buy the shares and the PEG pockets 300 million – and now owns 100% of the company. Not a bad result for a day's hustling and with no risk. Oh yeah, then the PEG charges the company management fees in the millions for doing this.

That's only the beginning though. In year 1 the company makes a 100 million again and they pay the banks the 80 million in loan repayments and they pay themselves a dividend (as they are the shareholders) of 20 million. Previously, the company would have paid the shareholders the 20 million dividend and had 80 million to help grow the company, invest in its future and put in the bank for a rainy day.

Year 2 is much the same, but profit drops to 90 million. The loan repayments of 80 million are made and 10 million goes to the PEG as a dividend.

Year 3. With no investment made in the company, revenues drop to 70 million. Now the company needs to borrow 10 million more in order to make its loan repayments. With so much debt however, this is much harder to do than initially. The company considers a sale but who wants to buy a company making 70 million a year (and going down) and 800 million of debt at a decent price? It's not a healthy company anymore. The PEG literally doesn't care. They've made 230 million risk-free in three years. If they can sell the company, even for 100 million, they make yet more money.

If the company is still remotely healthy, they may float it. Sell shares to the public. And yes, make even more money.

While PEG groups will claim that they add value to companies and realise their value, it's rarely true.[89] PEG people are number crunchers, they know nothing about running a company and 70% of companies that have been taken over by PEG groups have declined in value or closed down within three years of being taken over. But, the PEG's are heralded because they're rich. Private equity is nothing but financial manipulation.

Philip Green is a typical example. He bought Arcadia in 2002 for £850mn of other people's money and in October 2005 sent a cool £1.2bn (that's 1.2 billion pounds) as a tax-free dividend to his wife living offshore in Monaco - and he was knighted. Arcadia paid these dividends by borrowing the money and going further into debt. While for a spell, Green did invigorate the brands, Top Shop in particular, he wrecked the companies financially and left Arcadia with a £750mn pensions hole, which, thankfully, he'll have to help fill.

He did the same with BHS when he sold the company for £1 to a guy called Chappell, so he found himself in a difficult spot due to precedence. In the BHS situation Green was forced to contribute £363mn to the £570mn BHS pensions hole in order to retain his knighthood and stop court action. [90] Don't feel too sorry for him though, he was still net ahead by about £300mn as he'd paid himself well over £600mn over the years[91] and was still able, at the same time, to take delivery of his new £100mn yacht and £46mn jet – while thousands of staff received P45's. [92]

If he were forced to stump up £500mn now for the shortfall in the Arcadia pension pot, he'd still be up a good billion quid – again, no need to feel too sorry for him.

There are numerous examples of the results of PEG activities. Toys R Us had $1.86 billion in debt before its sale to a PEG and were $5 billion in debt after the PEG were running it; $3.2 billion to the PEG and $450mn in annual loan repayments to the company – and eventually the closure and loss of 30,00 jobs.[93]

Bottom line, this is a great racket (for some) if you can get into it. Let's look at a couple of other examples:

In 2004, Centrica owned the AA (Automobile Association) in the UK and they sold it to some PEG's for £1.75bn. The AA had no debt, 15mn members, turnover of £797mn and a profit of £93mn.[94] In 2014, the AA was floated at a valuation of £1.4bn. It had £3bn in debt, 13mn members, turnover of £970mn, a profit of £108mn and annual interest payments of £200mn.[95] And you know whose pockets the debt ended up in, plus the dividend payments (profits before being floated), plus management fees, plus over £500mn from the float? These PEG's took home close to £5bn, on a company whose value at its peak was £1.75bn. Oh yeah, and the same group was doing the same thing with Saga as they were doing with the AA.

A PEG group called Greybull Capital (an investment vehicle of a wealthy family) bought British Steel from Tata for £1 in June 2016. British Steel posted a loss of £19 million in 2018, while at the same time receiving up to £40 million from the UK business department. In March 2017, nine months after being bought by Greybull Capital, British Steel posted a profit of £47mn. Of course, Greybull said it was due to its remarkable skill at being turnaround specialists as it had posted a loss of £79mn in 2016. The reality is, large-scale steel contracts are signed long before delivery and receipt of funds. i.e., the contracts with Crossrail (for which British Steel supplied all the steel) and the Liverpool stadium etc., had been linked, long before Greybull appeared on the scene.

In early 2019, British Steel received a bridging loan of £120mn from the UK government and declared bankruptcy in May 2019 after talks for a further £30mn loan from the UK government fell through. This impacts 5,000 direct workers and 20,000 in the supply chain.

During this time, Greybull Capital was paid £9mn in management fees and £30mn in interest payments. There may be a pattern. Greybull rode in, to rescue Monarch Airlines in 2017, and walked away with £60mn, although Monarch closed, leaving 2,000 out of work and 100,000 stranded holidaymakers. And there was the Comet closure in 2012 and a £50mn payment after another PEG, OpCapita, was 'paid' over £50mn to turn it around.[96] To quote Nick Hood of Company Watch, 'OpCapita put very little of its own money at risk, behaving more like Comet's banker than its owner. They put in money, not as fixed share capital, but as loans.' He said, 'I think there is a moral issue here. The owners of this business took no risks (with their own money) but transferred them to suppliers and the staff – and the staff risk has been transferred to the government which is paying for the redundancy costs.'

This may all be legal – but it's wrong! Most of these PEG people know nothing about running businesses. They know spreadsheets. Numbers. Their numbers. And they are treated as heroes and sages because they are rich, when in fact they are actually destructive and taking away value rather than creating it. They wreck companies instead of creating them or 'turning them around'. PEG's are Takers, not Makers. They destroy jobs and communities rather than supporting jobs and communities. They are not to be applauded.

And now the PEG groups are going into property. Blackstone, the largest private equity group in the world, is also the largest landlord in the world. And get this, not just are they buying in blocks the 'social housing' part of developments in the UK, but they're also trying to say they're doing it for social good.[97] Do you believe them? Guess what they're doing with the rental incomes. They're packaging them up and selling them.[98] These investments are similar to mortgage bonds, but instead of mortgage payments, it's rental payments. If this sounds like 2008, that's because it is. This whole PEG scam needs shutting down. It is literally money for nothing and riches for free.

Let's see some pretty pictures courtesy of The Times that illustrates what happens in a typical PEG stock market floatation,[99] when the stock market as a whole is going up.

SAGA
Float 185p, May 2014
Thursday close 67¼ p
Backers Charterhouse Capital Partners, CVC Capital Partners and Permira through Acromas
Stake immediately after float **62%**
Stake today **0%**

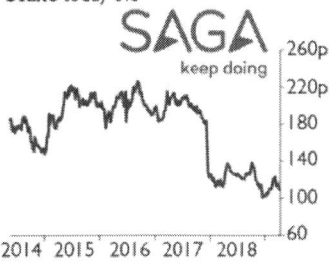

AA
Float 250p, June 2014
Thursday close 88½ p
Backers Charterhouse Capital Partners, CVC Capital Partners and Permira through Acromas
Stake post-float **4%**
Stake today **0%**

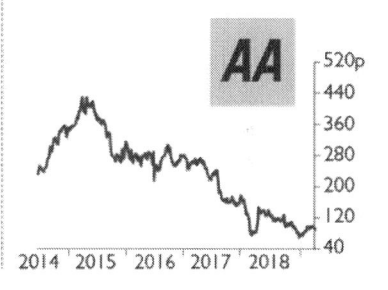

DEBENHAMS
Float 195p, May 2006
Thursday close 2p
Backers Texas Pacific, CVC Capital Partners and Merrill Lynch
Stake post-float **43%**
Stake today **0%**

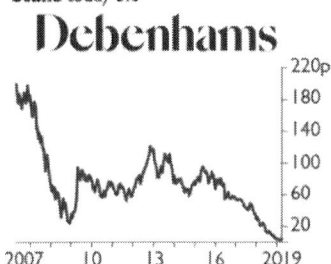

ASTON MARTIN LAGONDA
Float £19, October 2018
Thursday close £10.25¼p
Backers Investindustrial, Primewagon, Asmar and Adeem Automotive Manufacturing
Stake post-float **65.5%**
Stake today **46.5%**

80

Hedge Funds

Hedge Funds are financial alchemists, private investment groups that speculate with mega billions. Many began life by shorting markets using borrowed capital. They sold things they didn't have; with the expectation the price would go down and they could buy them back cheaply. Now they just legally steal. They borrow money, gear it up (this is when you '*leverage*' by being able to gamble $10 or more for every $1 they actually have), and speculate on anything they fancy. As with PEG groups, they are *not* investors. They are simply financiers playing with other people's money and making a fortune from it, regardless of whether they win or lose the bets they make. Typically, hedge funds take 2% of the money they manage in fees and 20% of the 'profits'. And if they have a bad year, they're not going to give the previous year's profits back.

Here's a stat for you: the twenty-five highest earning hedge fund managers in the US earned far more ($12.94 billion) than all the kindergarten teachers in the US combined ($8.6 billion), and they paid a lower tax rate.[100]

Think about that for a moment. Who adds real value and who's being rewarded? And the 'rewards' the hedge fund managers get, actually hurt the kindergarten teachers and everyone else.[101] Who would you rather see paid well: these twenty-five people or 160,000 kindergarten teachers?

The Workers

Investment bankers make very good money. The following graph is misleading though, in that it includes everyone in the securities industry who receives bonuses: secretaries, juniors and mid-level bankers. The reality is, many people made smaller amounts while some made millions in bonuses – as their investment firms were bailed out. Again.

The 30-year surge in Wall Street bonuses

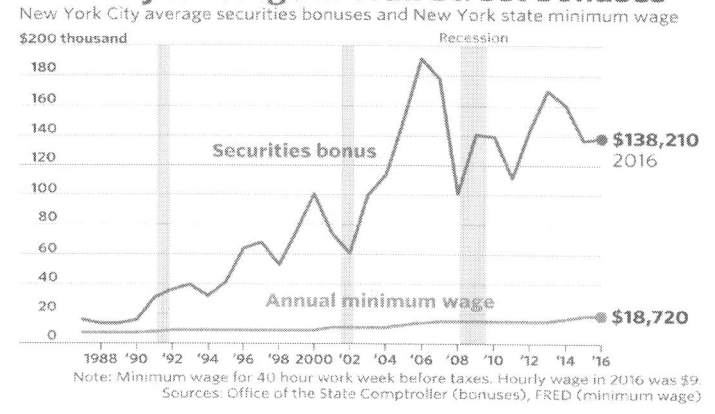

New York City average securities bonuses and New York state minimum wage

Securities bonus: $138,210 (2016)
Annual minimum wage: $18,720

Note: Minimum wage for 40 hour work week before taxes. Hourly wage in 2016 was $9.
Sources: Office of the State Comptroller (bonuses), FRED (minimum wage)

Including every secretary, teller, stockbroker and employee in 'finance', the industry that accounts for 4% of jobs in the US, now represents 7% of the economy (although they don't produce anything) and it takes 25% of all corporate profits.[102] $16 trillion of US household wealth was wiped out due to the Great Recession – and the financiers bought more assets from the middle classes at knock down prices and then rented them back. The Takers took even more.

Entrepreneurs on the other hand are Makers. Entrepreneurs are visionaries. Risk takers. We need them. Without them, we simply wouldn't be where we are today. They have the ideas. The energy. The balls. They are the adventurers of today. They envision tomorrow. They risk life and limb to bring an idea to fruition. They place heavy bets on the future. Most fail. Most successful entrepreneurs have started five businesses before they 'succeed', success being a monetary measure, at least in today's world. Was MySpace, one of the early Internet companies, a failure or did it lead to other great things?

Entrepreneurs should be rewarded for their risk. Most financially successful entrepreneurs have wealth because of the value they created in their company, their shares, not their salary. Often their salaries are quite low. Steve Jobs earned $1 a year, Jeff Bezos earns $81,000 in salary per year, and Bill Gates paid himself $900,000 in 2004. They have created their wealth through the businesses they make. They are to be applauded. They are Makers.

Sure, you may take issue with some of Amazon, the company's, practices, like paying no tax on $11 billion profit, in fact they got a tax credit but that's the fault of regulation, not Jeff Bezos. That's not to say I agree with the tax loopholes. I certainly don't.

When I refer to entrepreneurs, I include smaller local businesses, not just the household names we all know that become big. Whether it's a local restaurant, a bespoke clothing designer, a landscaper, hairdresser, coffee shop or florist, they all add value. They are Makers. They create products and deliver services that we need and want. They create jobs and support the local community. They add social value. Let's not forget, small businesses have traditionally accounted for about 50% of all employment. They take risk and have an enormous amount of stress to deal with, to follow their vision, their dreams. They should be applauded.

And then there are the **managers** who are paid to look after these businesses, keep them safe, and nurture them. Some individual managers are Makers, but often today, they are Takers with MBA's (Master of Business Administration).

Entrepreneurs are not to be confused with managers. Top managers at big companies are way overpaid. They simply aren't that valuable. I have trouble in my head justifying Mary Barra, the CEO of General Motors (GM), getting paid $24 million while GM is closing factories, firing 15,000 workers and moving factories abroad. That's 295 times higher than the average salaried GM worker receives – never mind the hourly workers. And this is a company that was bailed out by the US government ten years ago and given tax breaks in those states where the CEO is closing the factories. She simply does not add the same value of 1,000 workers at $240,000 a year or 5,000 workers at $48,000 a year. Seems wrong to me.

Managers manage. That's it, an important role, of course, but not unique. Top managers risk nothing and get huge rewards. But their company valuations haven't moved much. Since 1978, the salaries of CEO's in the US have risen ten times faster than wages – and that excludes the fringe benefits such as stock options, retirement plans, bonuses and private jets. In the UK, CEO's earned 180 times as much as the average worker, up from 47 times in 1998. In the US it's 300 times. In the US, median CEO pay is over $10 million and in the UK roughly $8 million.[103] Put this in perspective, by Jan 3 of this year (2020) a FTSE 100 CEO will have 'earned' more than the average yearly salary.[104] And don't forget, Jan

1 is a holiday, so it doesn't count. Are they really worth that much? Methinks not.

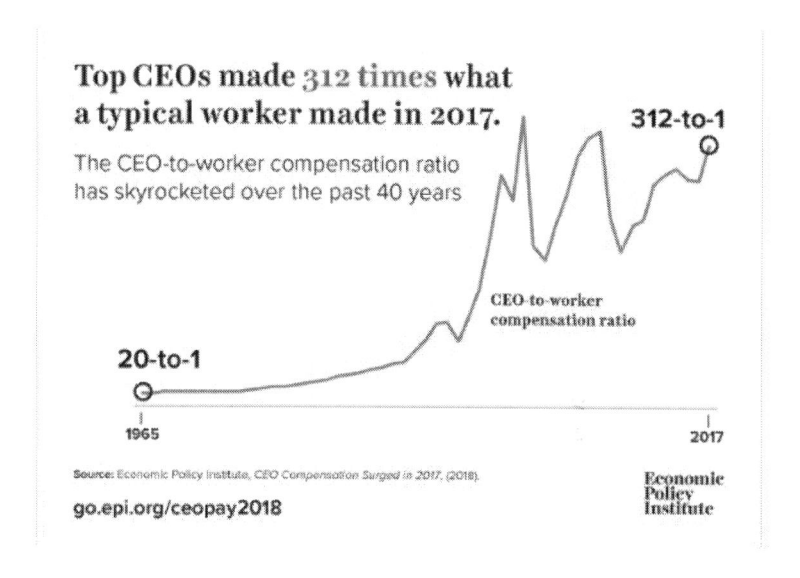

> **Top CEOs made 312 times what a typical worker made in 2017.**
>
> The CEO-to-worker compensation ratio has skyrocketed over the past 40 years
>
> 312-to-1
>
> CEO-to-worker compensation ratio
>
> 20-to-1
>
> 1965   2017
>
> Source: Economic Policy Institute, CEO Compensation Surged in 2017, (2018).
>
> go.epi.org/ceopay2018
>
> Economic Policy Institute

Today most top managers prefer to take by artificially inflating their company's share price, through share buybacks and dividend payments from debt, so that their stock options increase, rather than develop new products and services that open new markets.

And then there's **everyone else**. It's austerity and trickle-down economics for everyone else – and it's killing the middle classes. Trickledown economics is hurting.

Otherwise called voodoo economics by George Bush Snr., this is the ill-fated notion that lowering taxes will increase investment, help industry, create jobs, increase earnings and in the end, bring more money into the state coffers. It's a load of bollocks. In every example, whether on a national or regional level, the exact opposite happens.

When a billionaire makes another billion, what do they do? Do they buy more toys (yachts and Ferraris)? No. They already have more of those than they know what to do with. Do they invest in new start-ups? No.

They don't. Instead, they buy more existing assets. The super-rich buy more of the world's assets and rent them back to the general population. Nothing trickles down. In fact, the exact opposite happens.

- Tax receipts go down
- Social and government services suffer (everything from roadworks, to teachers and healthcare)
- Asset prices go up, real estate for example, and people end up having to rent from the super-rich, who now own the properties, rather than buying them themselves, as they are too expensive to afford
- Investment for new small businesses dries up
  Big companies get bigger and small companies, the traditional driver of new employment, are not started

Most people have not been benefitting from the rise in their productivity or the increase in global wealth. It's completely skewed to the rich. As an example, truckers made an average of $38,618 a year in 1980. If wages had just kept pace with inflation that would be over $114,722 today – but last year the average wage was $41,340.[105]

Disconnect between productivity and a typical worker's compensation, 1948–2014

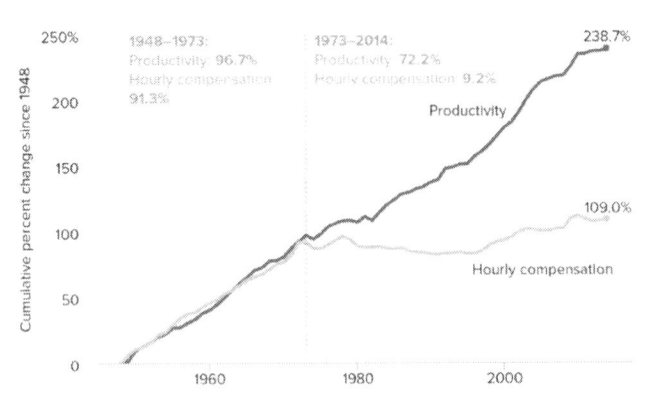

1948–1973:
Productivity: 96.7%
Hourly compensation: 91.3%

1973–2014:
Productivity: 72.2%
Hourly compensation: 9.2%

Productivity: 238.7%
Hourly compensation: 109.0%

Note: Data are for average hourly compensation of production/nonsupervisory workers in the private sector and net productivity of the total economy. "Net productivity" is the growth of output of goods and services minus depreciation per hour worked.

Source: EPI analysis of data from the BEA and BLS (see technical appendix for more detailed information)

Economic Policy Institute

In other words, it's not trickle-down, it's cascade-up – the rich get richer and the middle classes get poorer.

The super-rich, the 1% of the population, controls the bulk of global wealth. They use their capital to buy all the other assets out there (real estate, shares, bonds, cars, precious metals etc). The bottom 9% of the top 10% have a small portion of that capital and those assets, so are OK. The other 90%, with little or no capital, must use loans (money borrowed from the super-rich) to have things that the super-rich sell or rent out.

Money is not 'the root of all evil', but it is the root of almost everything. It shouldn't be. It should simply be an easy means of exchange. But now, money decides our lives. And the finance industry, that makes money without actually creating or making anything of value, runs the show. These financiers are legally stealing the wealth of the world – and destroying it at the same time.

I may be a capitalist but, as Marx pointed out, the downfall of capitalism will be capitalism itself. And right now, capitalism is teetering. Markets do not know best. And that's because the markets these days are run by lots of Takers, not Makers.

How We Got Into This Mess

The 'markets know best' theory led to the financial deregulation of the 70's, 80's and 90's which put finance back to the casino days of the 20's and justified tax cuts for the rich. It created the financial inequality that we see around us and, like all movements, was based around a theory: Neoliberalism.

Neoliberalism

Neoliberalism[106] has also been also called Reaganomics and is in fact trickle-down theory. Its premise is pretty straightforward, and although it is a proven failure, it is continuously resurrected. Basically, the theory is that the market knows best and will self-correct. It claims that there should be minimal regulation, minimal tax and minimal interference from the government, so that the markets can do what's best. Financial crashes are justified as just self-correction and government/taxpayer bailouts are too. Hmm, I don't think bailouts are supposed to be part of neoliberalism, the contrary in fact.[107]

Neoliberalism was used to justify financial deregulation and tax cuts. A 20th century conservative economist, named Art Laffer, believed in a magical tax rate at which he claimed people would stop working if they were taxed too much. And if you cut taxes for the rich, they would work longer, harder and better, and the fruits of their endeavours would trickle down to everyone else. Thing is, today most people work jobs that require them to be there, regardless of tax rate, and if they don't work, they won't receive any pay at all. As far as billionaires go, I can't see how billionaires are able to work more hours than already exist in a day, and they certainly aren't billions of times more productive than the rest of us.

Laffer sold the theory to Donald Rumsfeld and Dick Cheney in a bar in 1974. This was the foundation of Reaganomics. Incidentally, President Trump has just awarded Laffer the Presidential Medal of Freedom. [108] ...Although, that might have been because Laffer wrote a book called *Trumponomics*...

That's what Trump's tax cuts are: trickle down. These cuts helped create the biggest one-month deficit in US history at $234 billion.[109] Trump, who pledged to eliminate the US deferral debt in eight years, has actually increased it by more than $2 trillion in just two years, when the US economy is supposedly healthy.

Neoliberalism didn't work in the 70's, 80's, 90's and 2000's and it's certainly not working now.

Even after the Great Recession of 2008, nothing has changed. The financiers kept 'their' money and went back to business as usual. Even the $139 billion in fines imposed on banks between 2012 and 2014 had no impact. In fact, the derivatives market was 20% bigger in 2013 than in 2007 before the crash.[110] The fines were chump change to the financiers.

Financial Deregulation

As well as tax cuts, four important things happened on the financial deregulation front. Well, more than four of course, but for the purposes of what I'm writing, let's look at four.

Things changed in the 70's and 80's. But, first here's a quick explanation of some investment banking speak as everyone should be clear about two terms that are used frequently in banking: 'going long' and 'going short'.

Going long is fairly straightforward. You like something, like a share or bond, so you buy it and hold onto it. You hope it will rise in value and/or provide an income stream. You are making an investment in the future.

Going short is the opposite. It is selling a stock or bond you don't own with the expectation that the price will drop. If you plan on doing this for longer than a few hours you will need to find someone to borrow the shares or bonds from, to give to the person you sold them to.

As an example, you might think that the UK government is going to raise interest rates. If this were to happen, then government bonds would drop in price – remember the wings of an airplane? So, you decide to sell 100 bonds at £100 hoping those bonds will be worth less in the future. You sell the bonds, but you need to deliver (give) them to the buyer that you sold them to. What you do is 'borrow' the bonds from someone else. Say a pension fund. The pension fund loans you the 100 bonds for a month and you pay them a fee for this, so they make a little extra money on those bonds. By the end of the month, if things go as you planned, the bond price has dropped to £90, so you actually finally buy the 100 bonds in the market (cover your short) and make £10, minus what you paid the pension fund to lend them to you.

The four changes:

The first is that investors were allowed to sell shares they didn't own (to go 'short'). Previously, only market makers could do this, in order to maintain a market in a share, and would close the 'short' position out as soon as possible. This is a big part of what happened with 'Big Bang' (1986) in the UK: deregulation of the financial markets. Again, lots more went on, but one of the far-reaching changes was being able to 'short' a share if you felt it would go down in price. Investment groups calling themselves hedge funds were born. Their speciality was 'betting' against companies, not investing in companies.

Hedging used to mean removing uncertainty by using futures and options (hence the name hedge funds), where 'hedge' implies minimising risk. It used to be about selling next month's corn harvest at a price agreed upon today (selling something you don't have yet) or buying next month's oil at a price agreed today. But hedge funds aren't hedging anything, they are simply betting by selling something they don't have. And yes, even they call it 'betting'.

The second was the repeal of the Glass-Steagall Act in the US. This was introduced in 1933 after the stock market crashes of the 20'/30's. It separated retail banking from investment banking. By repealing the law, retail banks were allowed to use their balance sheets to 'invest' in or bet on the markets. And, they didn't just bet $1 for every $1 dollar they had. They 'geared' up and invested $10 or more for every $1 they had on their balance sheets, the balance sheets of the retail banks being all the money on deposit with the bank. So, many retail banks went into investment banking because shareholders wanted better returns on their investments and bankers wanted bonuses.

This saw a return to the roulette of the roaring 20's. The financial markets became a casino. It was all about betting other people's money. Those that did, made fortunes and were heralded as sages. They didn't make or create anything though. They gambled. They took. Of course, this all came home to roost in the 2008 crash. And the governments paid the bill and taxpayers and small investors lost out.

The 80's were the time of Gordon Gekko and 'greed is good'. And yes, I fell for it and moved to the UK from the US to be a part of Big Bang – a teeny inconsequential part I might add. Although I did 'borrow' a third of the entire long maturity, dated bonds of the Spanish government bond market, but that's another story…. My employer made a fortune. To note, bonds with longer maturity dates have wider price swings than bonds with shorter maturity dates, so speculators love them.

The third thing was the lifting of caps on interest rates, so debt became a real money maker and a major instrument of finance. In the 80's, credit card interest rates went to over 20%, Michael Milken and 'junk' bonds arrived and it was the era of Ronald Reagan – who entered office in Jan 1981 with the US as the largest creditor nation in the world and left office in Jan 1989 with the US as the largest debtor nation in the world. In the span of eight years Reagan turned things upside down and the debt age truly began. And in the UK, Margaret Thatcher spent the national assets of the UK buying elections, rather than investing in the future of the country. In Japan things were so crazy that at one point the Imperial Palace in central Tokyo was worth more than all the real estate in California. [111] Everything changed.

Today, companies are borrowing money to pay shareholder dividends and to do share buybacks (buyback their own shares) as it drives prices up, and stock markets. They even do this when they have cash – offshore as it's more tax efficient. Think about this. Apple has almost $300 billion cash sitting offshore (it doesn't want to bring it onshore and pay tax) but has borrowed almost $100 billion in the past two years to pay shareholder dividends and buy its own shares back.[112] In 2015 alone, US companies paid over $1 trillion to shareholders in share buybacks and dividends, while wages remained flat.[113]

Companies who don't have the cash offshore are also doing this. They are going further and further into debt to pay shareholder dividends. Yet, because they are paying dividends, the share price is going up, which means, you guessed it, they can borrow more to pay more dividends. And we all know how this will end – crash, government bailout, 'austerity' for normal people, rich getting richer, middle classes getting poorer.

Much of the wealth of the super-rich has been fuelled by debt, the debt of the bottom 90% who need to borrow to buy and rent things that the super-rich sell and rent to them. And let's not forget the taxpayer-funded government borrowing that's needed to support the super-rich casino games.

The fourth item is derivatives. Warren Buffet, the world's most famous investor and periodically the world's richest person, says 'derivatives are financial weapons of mass destruction'. He's right of course. He invests by going long and often holds onto shares in companies for decades.

Someone pays a fee to guarantee that they can buy or sell something in the future at a price fixed today. This is a useful financial tool as you can reduce uncertainty by paying to fix a price today, to hedge against future price fluctuations.

Futures can be important and useful instruments and the biggest futures exchange is in Chicago. They were primarily used for physical goods, commodities – crops, animal stock, oil, minerals etc. We'll address these first.

Imagine you're a wheat farmer. You'd like to sell next year's harvest at today's price to remove the uncertainty of what the actual price may be in the future. You know your costs next year and will make a profit, so you are willing to pay today to guarantee that profit. It makes life more certain for you. You are willing to give up the chance that the price of wheat goes up and you could make more money by neutralising the risk that the price of wheat may go down and you could lose your shirt. You are not a speculator or gambler after all, you're a farmer. You want to guarantee, to set tomorrow's price today. You want to hedge the risk.

On the other side of this equation is a bread manufacturer. They are happy with today's price of wheat and they can make a profit at this price without having to raise the price of bread to their customers. Sure, they could make more money or charge their customers less for a loaf of bread if the price of wheat went down, but they could also be forced to pay more and raise prices if the price of wheat went up. They would rather remove the risk of the price of wheat in the future and hedge themselves by buying tomorrow's wheat at a price agreed today. They have price certainty. After all, they are not speculators or gamblers, they are bread makers – they want to guarantee, to set tomorrow's price today.

As you can see, this makes a lot of sense. It removes future uncertainty. You pay to hedge the future.

Then, there are options. They are similar to futures with one big difference. They are not based around something physical, but rather around a financial instrument. They are based around shares and bonds. They give someone the ability to buy or sell a share or bond in the future, at a price agreed upon today.

For instance, an insurance company may know it will need to sell some shares in the future to meet some outflows due to some large upcoming insurance claims. These outflows can be met at today's price and they would prefer to remove the uncertainty of tomorrow's price. They buy an option to sell the shares at today's price.

Conversely, perhaps a pension fund has funds coming in monthly and would like to buy shares in a company they like. They like today's price as it gives them a certain return, so because they would like to fix tomorrow's price today, they buy an option doing exactly that.

The reality though is that derivatives quickly became speculative instruments and ever more complicated. People used options to bet on price movements by buying or selling options. And they went from being based on shares and bonds to interest rates, stock indexes and more. Then, the financiers hired PhD mathematicians and physicists and derivatives became very, very complicated. They began to combine all types of things together and to create new derivatives that could be based on anything, such as the $/£ exchange rate vs. the price of gold vs. the length of women's skirts (why not) vs. the price of wheat futures.

Derivatives are complicated financial machinations that no one understands, even probably the people who wrote them. Derivatives take options to a whole new level by creating financial instruments based around lots of variables. So many in fact, that no one actually knows who's liable for what. Which is what happened in 2008.

If you really want to know what caused the crash of 2008 watch The Big Short.[114] It was due to derivatives based around dodgy home loans.

In a nutshell, a bunch of investment bankers invented a new game of pass the parcel based on 'derivatives' around home loans. These were called CDO's (Collateralized Debt Obligation). Retail bankers loaned easy money for over-valued homes, to people who couldn't afford them. These loans were bundled with other loans, repackaged and resold to investors as CDO's.

Some retail banks got rid of their risk and made money by selling the loans to investment banks that packaged them up and sold them to investors. Some banks formed just to give out these risky subprime mortgages and earn fees by selling them to the investment banks.

The credit rating on these loans would be very low (subprime) if they were marketed by themselves so in order to sell them, the investment bankers dressed them up by including them with other loans and having someone else guarantee them.

Investment bankers convinced other retail banks, and insurance companies like AIG in particular (at the time the world's largest insurance company with $1 trillion in assets), to guarantee these subprime instruments by using their balance sheets and a derivative that is called a 'Credit Default Swap'. They made the subprime loans look better to investors than they were – claiming they removed risk for investors. Investors were betting on AIG, not the subprime loans. AIG made money by agreeing to let investment banks use their balance sheets. AIG thought they were safe. They weren't. To add insult to injury, AIG invested some of their fees and profits into, yes you guessed it, subprime mortgages.[115] They'd thought it was easy money.

The subprime loan wasn't what was on the table to investors; it was AIG everyone was looking at. This combined with rating agencies that gave these loans very high safety investment ratings, due to AIG, were essentially a charade. The credit agencies did not look closely at the underlying loans.

The banks made fees and investment bankers made a fortune buying and selling these instruments to investors – until homeowners stopped making payments. The subprime loans lost their value and AIG and others had to stump up. It was the end of AIG, which received an $85bn bailout from the US government.[116] Similarly, General Electric (GE) became a huge financial player by lending money. GE settled with the US government with a fine of $1.5bn in 2019 for its involvement in a subprime mortgage bank it had owned, but luckily sold, before everything went tits up.[117]

The market crashed and AIG, and others who guaranteed the loans or were giving subprime loans, went bust. And the government and taxpayers bailed them out. Governments around the world printed money like there was no tomorrow and called it 'quantitative easing'. Trillions of dollars were printed and used to purchase bonds so as to stop a 1920's type crash.

The investment bankers, who were responsible for this, were all laughing in their beach houses, which they kept. And then, as ordinary people suffered through 'austerity' and had no money, the rich bought all the cheap assets. They were the only ones with cash.

All this needs to be reined in and put in check otherwise it will happen again. And again.

How Do We Fix This Sh*t?

Sometimes, when things get too complicated, we need to step back and start from scratch, to simplify things. We need to go back to basics and decide what the actual objectives are. And then we need to go about setting up as simple processes as possible to achieve them.

Let's all be clear on what the most important things are, the basics: people and the environment or more specifically, the welfare of people and the future of the environment. This is what it's all about. Protecting and nurturing humanity and the world around us are the goals. Ruining one or the other is plain old bad for all of us.

The first thing we need to do is rethink our relationship with money, how we 'earn' it, who has it and essentially what it represents. We need to reverse financial inequality and have money represent the value of people and the environment.

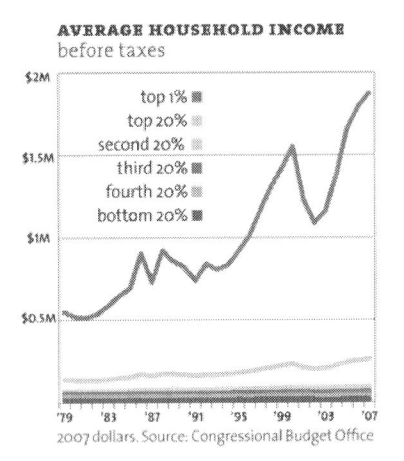

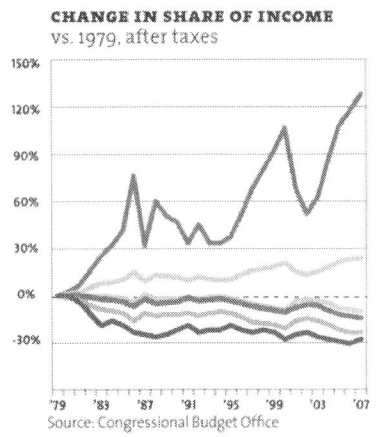

AVERAGE HOUSEHOLD INCOME
before taxes
2007 dollars. Source: Congressional Budget Office

CHANGE IN SHARE OF INCOME
vs. 1979, after taxes
Source: Congressional Budget Office

Banking and finance are very important – once you strip out the roulette wheel component (the gambling). But the money distribution is all wrong. The people of least social value, the gamblers using other people's money, have the most money, while the most important workers, teachers, nurses etc. receive the least.

If we are going to value people's contributions properly then we must correct these money imbalances, imbalances caused by runaway and unchecked capitalism where the only important thing is money. Particularly as a lot of that money is made from other's people debt and misery. In many ways, the US represents the best and the worst of this.

The US has become the world's first 'poor rich country'. Get your head around this stat: the average American, 73% of the US population, now dies $61,000 in debt, and that excludes burial costs.[118] Americans are some of the hardest and most productive workers in the world. They work their entire lives, with very few holidays, yet when they die, they go out 'worth' less than when they came in.[119] It is simply not right for them to die less 'valuable' than when they were born, after a lifetime of work. I think you'd have to be a cruel, sadistic narcissist to think this is remotely fair.

The most common debts are mortgages, credit cards, car loans, student loans and medical. People had to borrow money for the basics – housing, transport, education and health. Debt accrued by normal, average people trying to do nothing more than survive, has made the top 1% super-rich.

Step One - Show Me The Money

To make any real positive changes we need to get rid of the financial inequality that currently exists and curtail the casino financial markets and the financiers. Many wealthy people realise it's in their self-interest to do this as well. They know that if they don't, there could be tremendous social unrest and they need to protect themselves, before things get completely out of hand.

Finance Regulation

The crash of 2008 resulted in huge bailouts of banks and insurance companies. Citigroup, one of the leading advocates of deregulation for many years, was a central player. Deemed 'too big to fail', it received $476 billion from the US government.[120]

Even Sandy Weill, the person who created Citigroup and espoused financial deregulation with fervour, startled the financial world when he had an epiphany in July 2012, and declared that he thought retail banking and investment banking should once again be separated.[121] He's right. It is well past time to separate retail banking from investment banking, to separate the restaurant from the casino again – and keep it that way. Or, should I say this way:

- **Retail banking.** Back to its roots, taking deposits and making loans
- **Investment banking.** Bring the market makers back and curtail 'shorting' from being an investment strategy. If you like a stock or bond buy it (go long). If you don't like it, don't buy it. This would kill a lot of the volatility that the casinos like. Financiers don't care if stocks and bonds go up or down, just that they move
- **Derivatives market**. Regulate very strictly and get rid of instruments no one understands. Not being able to short the market will help quash derivatives – but not totally
- **Interest rates.** Cap at 15%

Basically, we need to bring some regulation back to the markets and limit the casino.

Financial Inequality

Financial inequality is not created by the markets alone but also by government action, or inaction, in other areas.

Wealth and income inequality are the first things that need addressing and ironically, without changing much, they can be addressed under today's existing mechanisms.

Two areas, that if addressed differently could reduce stress significantly, decrease costs and increase efficiency across the board, are tax and UI (Universal Income). They both require a complete rethink, as does GDP (Gross Domestic Product). The reality is, we are the economy. Consumer spending is what generates GDP – it's 70% of the economy. No factory makes chairs or widgets for the hell of it; they make them to sell to us. They want our money. Likewise, services people perform have a value and our economies are long past being about just physical production. Services account for a huge portion of GDP, 80% in the UK and US.

Even from the perspective of the people who own the factories and services that deploy AI, it would be very short sighted to not ensure that people have money. After all, who would then be able to buy the products and services of companies if people have no money? Henry Ford pointed this out when asked about why he paid his workers a minimum wage of $5 an hour in 1914.

"It is not the employer who pays the wages. Employers only handle the money. It is the customer who pays the wages."

He recognised that he would increase staff retention (it costs time to train people) and he would also be paying them enough money to buy their own cars.

That's $120 an hour in today's money,[122] which is a hell of a long way from the $7.25 minimum wage in the US and £8.21 in the UK.

In other words, if the super-rich who own the companies don't wake up, eventually they won't have any customers. The super-rich can save their own hides by advocating Universal Incomes and paying into this system, like Henry Ford. BTW, almost everyone thought Ford was crazy at the time.

The trend is clear. Cutting taxes negatively impacted the bottom 90% of the population while it enriched the top 1% of the USA and hurt the country. Cutting taxes gave oxygen to narcissist dictators and financiers.

Income inequality in the USA, 1970-2014

Pre-tax national income | Bottom 50% | Share | ADULTS | EQUAL SPLIT
Pre-tax national income | Top 1% | Share | ADULTS | EQUAL SPLIT

Hang on a sec. What about if we'd done trickle-up instead of trickle-down to sort out the mess of 2008? Let's see how that might have played out.

Austerity or Trickle-Up?

Since 2008, households have had to endure 'austerity' to pay for the government bailout of financial institutions and the financiers. Households have increased their debt to survive, social services have been cut and the gap between the super-rich and middle class grew like it was on steroids. Why? We might wonder. The answer is straightforward. It's that trickle-down theory again.

You see, the central banks decided that if they printed more money, $3.7 trillion in the US and £445 billion in the UK, and used that money to buy back bonds from the rich, then the rich would invest and spend this money and this would stimulate the economy and stop a crash like in the 1920's. They called it 'quantitative easing' instead of trickle-down, but it's essentially the same thing. And the results were the same. The rich got richer and bought more assets and the middle classes got poorer and had to borrow more money from the rich to simply stay afloat. Here's a nice image courtesy of the BBC to illustrate the quantitative easing theory and it looks suspiciously like trickle-down economics. Thank you Gordon Brown, the Labour politician who made all this possible and 'saved' the world.

Quantitative Easing: The theory

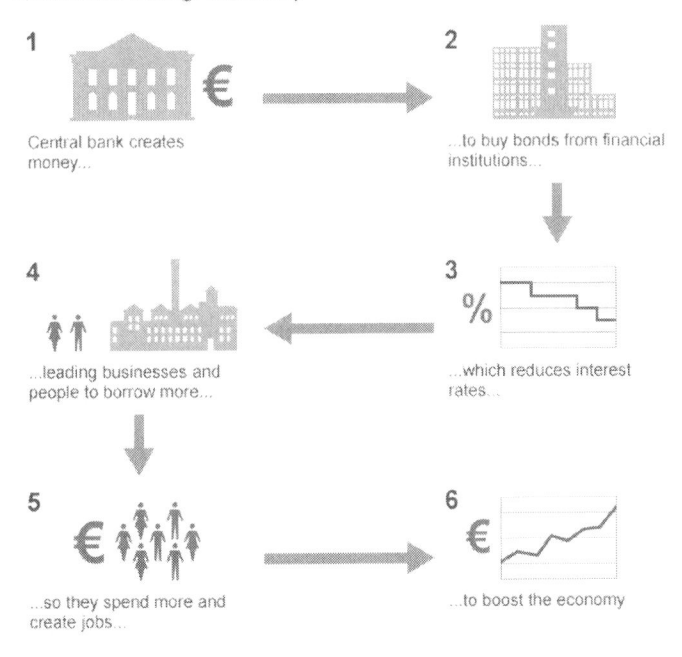

1. Central bank creates money...
2. ...to buy bonds from financial institutions...
3. ...which reduces interest rates...
4. ...leading businesses and people to borrow more...
5. ...so they spend more and create jobs...
6. ...to boost the economy

This theory didn't really pan out well. Austerity happened for most of the population and wealth inequality increased.

We know that 70% of the economy is being driven by consumer spending. If the goal was to boost the economy (picture #6), then surely stimulating consumer spending should have been the objective. Seems to me, the rational thing to have done, would have been to stimulate spending by consumers, trickle-up economics.

But, what would have happened had trickle-up been the route taken instead of trickle-down? People would have spent more money; government tax revenues would have been up; jobs would have been created; government services would not have been cut and austerity would have been avoided.

Let's play with the exact same amount of money that the governments spent on quantitative easing so that we have a fair comparison and see what would have happened. Like-for-like spending. That's £445 billion in the UK and $3.7 trillion in the US.

First, how could the government have motivated people to spend more? Here's an idea. Total UK consumer debt today, including student loans, is £428 billion in the UK and $4 trillion in the US. The governments could have used that same quantitative easing money and paid off the ENTIRE country's consumer debt, student loans, credit cards, auto loans and personal loans. Just imagine, no more debt. Without going back into debt, consumers would have had more money to spend, simply because they wouldn't have been making loan repayments. I reckon that would have put a smile on many people's faces and they would have been out there spending – boosting the economy. Wow. I can imagine that that would have kick-started some serious consumer spending. The opposite of austerity would have happened.

And where would that quantitative easing money have gone? To the retail banks, the ones that lend money to real people and real businesses. The retail banks would have had money in the till. They could then have started lending money to businesses that would then have had money to expand and invest in the future.

Using the images in the trickle-down theory, let's look at it in reverse.

Start at step 1, we need the money after all, but then let's go to step 6 and work backwards to step 3. We'll skip step 2, as I'll explain.

6) Consumer spending would have boosted the economy
5) This would have created more jobs and enticed businesses to expand and invest more
4) Lending to businesses would have increased
3) Interest rates could have gone down, if they even needed to, as banks would have been flush

The only thing missing is step 2, 'buy bonds from financial institutions', i.e. buying bonds from investment banks – in other words, buying bonds from the financiers who created the crisis in the first place.

What would *not* buying the bonds have meant? Some investment banks would have gone tits up and the financiers wouldn't have had the taxpayers picking up their gambling tab. And, of course, they wouldn't have been able to keep on gambling so easily. As well as this, the widening gap between the super-rich and the middle-classes would have slowed down. Result. I doubt many of us would have been shedding a tear for the financiers.

Hmm, trickle-up economics sounds pretty good. Wish we'd done that, so we didn't end up with this.

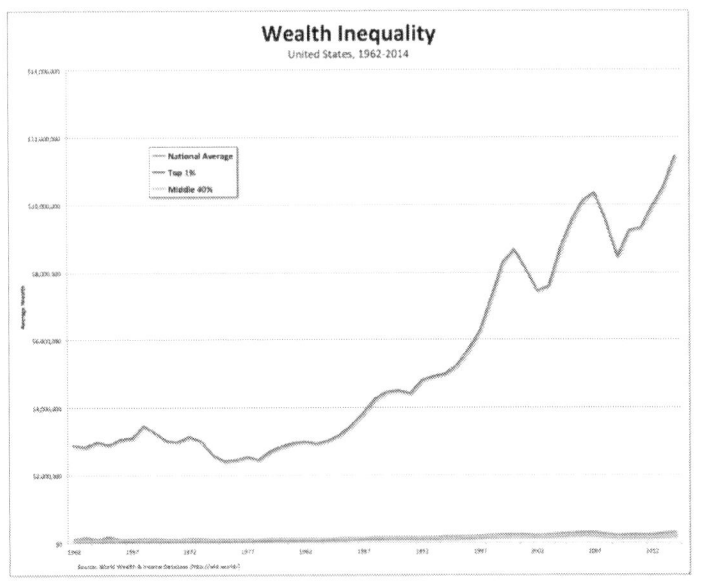

Wealth Inequality
United States, 1962-2014

Trickle-down economics simply does not work. You can only have so many Ferraris, masseuses, personal trainers, houses, gardeners and yachts. After that, the extra money is used to buy the world's assets. It does NOT trickle-down. It gushes up into a few people's pockets.

Trickle-down does the opposite of what it says on the tin. It reduces investment and consumer spending – it actually *hurts* the economy. As Billionaire investor, Nick Hanauer pointed out in his controversial TED talk, 'Businesses and the rich do not create jobs. Jobs are created by a feedback loop between customers and businesses that is set in motion by consumers increasing their demand.'[123]

You have to wonder how people come up with such obviously lame ideas like trickle-down. Perhaps they know it is a bad idea, but they just need a justification for taking more. Just a thought.

You know what the financiers would have been saying to an idea like this? It would be, 'this is socialist and we'd be rewarding people for getting into debt'.

What the financiers are really trying to say is that taxpayers paying off the financiers' gambling debts, the debts that got them their toys and almost brought down the financial system, is fine. It's capitalism. Yet, taxpayers paying off all of a country's loans in one go – student loans, credit cards and payday loans, but not yacht loans, I might add – so they can boost the economy, is presented as socialist. That's nuts. Millions of people would have disposable income and breathe a sigh of relief.

The financier gamblers were the ones who were rewarded for bad behaviour. Perhaps we should have let them fail and lose their beach houses.

Austerity is the result of trickle-down economics and financiers. We must sort this out, as financial inequality is a threat to democracy and capitalism.

Tax – The New Social

Tax is necessary. I'm sure that we can all agree that security, roads, the environment, education, health, legal and welfare are very important. Tax is what allows a country to provide the infrastructure that people need. The proper use of tax creates an environment that helps businesses starting up and makes it safe to walk down the street. Tax allows us to create opportunities for ourselves and protect our society.

But, we all cringe when we hear the world 'tax'. It has as many negative connotations as the word 'politician'. It's something to be avoided and minimised. This is because throughout history, and in Level 1 and Level 2 countries still, the money went into a few people's back pockets. And in Level 3 and Level 4 countries, we've been told that capitalism works best with low taxes, that low taxes stimulate growth. Added to that, we don't feel it's fair because of the gap between the super-rich and the middle-classes. We feel we're not benefitting from what we feel we paid for. The average Scandinavian, where there are good social services, does not think tax is bad compared to someone in the UK or the US. That's because while they have a high tax rate, they benefit more from it. It removes stress. They see what they get in return for it.

Let's change our thinking and call it what it is, a contribution to our society. Without it there would be no police, roads, schools, health and social services. It's a society fund that maintains the infrastructure of the country we live in. We should be proud to contribute to our 'society'. Rather than trying to pay less to our society we should want to contribute more – and I don't just mean in pounds and pence. Tax does not need to be high, as long as everyone pays their fair share, which is not the case now.

We need to change our thinking on it. Let's start by ditching the negative connotations associated with the word tax. Let's call it social and think about it as a contribution to the society fund. It already sounds better, contributing to the society fund, rather than paying tax. And we need to make tax fairer. Let's evolve and simplify tax.

Personal Tax

Wouldn't life be far simpler if there was one social rate for everything and everyone – a simple, flat tax? No deductions for this, that and the other. No complicated formulas. No complicated tax returns. Let's say 25% tax on incomes up to say $10 million and then 50% social thereafter. Seems fair.

When you earn, you contribute 25% of what you earn to the common cause – the society fund. There are no tax loopholes and no reasons for the rich to pay accountants and lawyers to get around the rules – rules they created.

None of this is radical. Countries change tax rates all the time and several countries already have flat-rate taxes of 20 to 25%. Ten states in the US already have a flat-tax rate and in the UK the Institute for Economic Affairs wants one at 15%,[124] and the Institute of Directors and the TaxPayers' Alliance is promoting it too.[125] This is in no way a radical idea; it's just a change in tax rates.

This is what Rory Meakin of the Taxpayers Alliance told the BBC:

> *Britain's tax code is one of the longest in the world. Tolley's yellow and orange tax handbooks*

now extend to over 17,000 pages, three times longer than in 1997.

We have a basic rate, a higher rate and an additional rate of income tax, with a different set of rates for dividends and yet another for savings.

And then there's National Insurance, with different thresholds and rates for each, and separate rates for share fishermen, overseas development workers, the self-employed and women married before some time in 1977.

There's no need for taxes to be so maddeningly complex.

That complexity isn't just maddening, either. It also makes the tax system both economically and socially destructive. Quite apart from the money it sucks out of the productive economy, it's economically damaging for two reasons.

First, it requires an army of clever accountants and tax lawyers to navigate the system for businesses and an opposing battalion of bureaucrats to monitor all those rules and rates.

Second, it means that the public just doesn't understand how the tax system operates, which, among other things, risks discouraging people with new commercial ideas from starting new businesses. That means opportunities are lost and fewer jobs are created.

And it's socially damaging because the confusion leads to suspicion that others are getting away with something, directly leading to distrust of the whole system.

We need to sweep away all that complexity and replace it with lower, simpler and more proportionate taxes, which are easier to understand, with fewer loopholes and exemptions

Meakin is absolutely right but beware of a wolf in sheep's clothing. Many of the people advocating flat taxes, including Meakin, are right-wingers and want one very low rate for everyone, like 15%. They use the trickle-down argument to justify it. As we know, trickle-down doesn't work, but trickle-up does, so we need two rates: 25% up to $10 million (£8 million UK) and then 50%.

Here's a simple graph that shows what trickle-down tax cuts have done in the US. The graph only runs through 2009, after which tax rates for the super-rich continued to decrease to 20%, where they are now. The two trajectories exactly mirror the widening gap between the super-rich and the middle-classes and the increase in the amount of money the government borrows. Look at the period between 1980 and 1990 when Reagan and trickle economics really kicked off, a period that saw the US go from being the largest creditor nation in the world, to the largest debtor nation in the world.

Average Tax Rates for the Highest-Income Taxpayers, 1945-2009

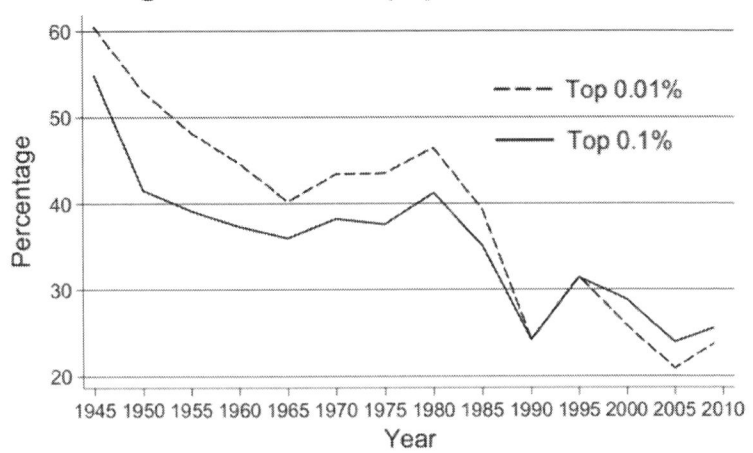

Source: CRS calculations using Internal Revenue Service (IRS) Statistics of Income (SOI) information.

Taxes used to be far higher at the top end in the US, up to 70%. As is clear, life has gotten worse for the middle-classes and the financial inequality has widened as top tax rates were dropped. Trickle-down simply does not work and this has been proven. Most people back a higher rate of tax for the top 1%. It's been done before. A top flat rate of 50% tax would stop this financial inequality gap from widening and reduce the need for the country to borrow.

Couple that with Inheritance tax changes, and we'll evolve and be in equilibrium in less than a generation.

Inheritance Tax

Inheritance tax is very important. We all want to leave something for our children, and we should be able to. Let me reiterate though, the problem is neither the upper middle classes, who make hundreds of thousands of dollars a year, nor the rich, who make millions of dollars a year. It's the super-rich, who make hundreds of millions and billions, and pay almost no tax.

People who inherit vast fortunes are a different matter. Often, they haven't earned anything themselves. Don't get me wrong. Some are amazing philanthropists who contribute to society and good causes. Great. Many though contribute little of social value to society.

Children of wealthy families grow up with every opportunity possible; great educations, lives, toys, networks and opportunities. But when they turn eighteen, they should be treated like everyone else. Well almost. We all work for our children after all, and we should be able to help them, within reason. Bill Gates agrees, as do many other very wealthy people who aren't leaving all their fortunes to their kids – well, only a part, but not all. The kids are being provided for. Bill Gates' kids are not going to be billionaires through inheritance; they will *only* inherit $10 million each.[126]

And Warren Buffet famously said, "I still believe in the philosophy ... that a very rich person should leave his kids enough to do anything, but not enough to do nothing."[127]

Sure, a motivation of parents is to provide for their children, but there should be a maximum that can be inherited from an estate as a whole and a maximum per person. The question is: how do we set this amount?

If everyone has a minimum income or UI (Universal Income), which we'll discuss later, we could use UI as the basis for maximum inheritance levels. Let's see how that could play out with a UI of £12,000 per year.

If one person could inherit up to 1,000 (years) x UI and in this case it would be £12 million, the maximum that could be inherited by any one person would be £12 million.

For the estate maximum as a whole, let's multiply this (£12 million) by 10, so there's plenty to share. So, in this case, the maximum that could be inherited from an estate would be £120 million.

£12 million per person tax free, coupled with the UI, that should keep them in clover for the rest of their lives.

So, what happens to the rest? It gets split. Half goes to the government of the day as social; the other half goes to the sovereign wealth fund (as discussed later).

Let's look at a £1.2 billion UK estate example to see the breakdown:

£12 million maximum per recipient
= 1,000 (years) x £12,000 (UI)

£120 million maximum per estate
= 10 (inheritors) x £12 million

Balance: £1.08 billion
= £1.2 billion (total estate) - £120 million (inheritance)

Balance split: = £1.08 billion / 2 = £540 million

£540 million - social to the government

£540 million - social investment to the SWF

Easy. Inheritance tax solved and even the super-rich will want a decent UI. No more super-rich from inheritance though. They'll have to earn it!

There shouldn't be any caps on wealth earned. Inventors and entrepreneurs are the backbone of our society and their potential incomes should not be capped, nor should they pay more tax than others. Whether it's new products and services or space exploration, we don't want to stifle this. Today, space exploration is partially driven by private fortunes such as Elon Musk and SpaceX. We should applaud this and not stifle this. We need trail blazers – whether to climb mountains, go to space, invent or invest in new health devices or develop new goods and services.

These measures will help reduce tax evasion, but more is needed.

Let's put a stop to tax evasion in a very simple manner, keep it simple. Imagine how much easier it would be to complete your tax returns if there were no exemptions and a flat-rate tax.

If you were a resident of a country, you would file a return in that country. Residents would then pay tax dependent on where they spent their time. If they split their time between two countries, the tax would get split proportionally between the two.

It's more than fair and makes it easier to deal with supposed offshore investors.

Offshore Investors

Currently non-resident companies and people do not pay tax on their investments in the UK or the US. Why? Simple. As they're not 'resident' they're not taxed. But, this is of no benefit whatsoever to the country.

Offshore businesses are used as vehicles of the super-rich and international companies, to avoid paying tax. They influence politicians to keep it that way by claiming it's good for the local economy and by funding their re-election campaigns. Politicians will tell voters that these breaks attract investment. They don't. Investment is what VC's (Venture Capitalists) do. This is buying assets, pure and simple, like shares, bonds and real estate (which pushes up prices for locals). In fact, UK economists reckon that focusing on finance cost the UK £4.5 trillion between 1995 and 2015, and UK GDP is now 14% lower because of this focus.[128] It does not benefit the local economies, as politicians and financiers would have us believe. It actually damages local economies by distorting asset prices.

Non-resident companies and people should pay tax like everyone else. The super-rich and companies can either put their money in local investments and pay tax or they can keep it under their mattresses and earn nothing and go live in the Cayman Islands. It's a simple choice.

The super-rich and the rich have some $30 trillion sitting offshore. These tax mechanisms can be used to finally tax the super-rich. If they are citizens of a country and reside there, or make money there, then they should behave as such and carry their weight. If they don't, they can live offshore.

In the case of Philip Green's wife, who I mentioned earlier, she would have had to pay 50% tax on most of that £1.2 billion dividend. Even if she'd used an offshore company it would have been taxed, which is much better than the £0 actually received by the UK taxman.

I need to point out here that these taxes are not unique, nor do they take away the wealth of the rich. They would still be as obscenely rich as they are now. What these taxes do though is begin the process of naturally correcting the imbalances. The rich will start to pay the taxes they should have been paying all along – the taxes mere mortals pay. These taxes will stop this slide into wealth inequality that we are witnessing now, raise much needed funds in Social Tax, and coupled with inheritance tax changes, put things back on a more even keel. Bit-by-bit, year-by-year, until twenty years from now, we will have removed the most glaring wealth and income inequality.

Now we've dealt with the personal tax side of financial inequality, time to look at the corporates. Interestingly, tax is similar to currencies. Countries, states/provinces and cities use it proactively to attract people and businesses to them, which negatively impacts the other areas.

That's what an offshore tax haven is. It's a country or territory that doesn't charge taxes on money that is generated outside of its jurisdiction, whether generated by a company or a person. It makes money by charging for related admin services. This is what people mean when they refer to 'offshore money'.

Then, there are grade two tax dodges. These are places that offer very low tax rates to attract companies and the super-rich, but *do* charge a tax, so they are clean and not offshore. Ireland is a popular example these days. It's popular because it charges a corporate tax rate of 12% but is considered legitimate.

Ideally, everywhere would have the same tax rates. But that's not the case. While we've addressed personal tax, we need to address the corporate tax situation as well.

Company Tax

One of the reasons the big multinational companies and the super-rich pay little tax is that they are taxed on profits and they fictionally reduce these profits by moving money offshore in a process known as 'transfer pricing' (explained next). They can do this as companies are taxed on profits, not income. Being priced on profits, not income, also allows big companies to strangle small companies by offering products and services for 'free' or at abnormally low costs. They kill competition, which stifles innovation.

Think about Amazon. It's the world's fourth most valuable company, sometimes third, but really there's little in it. It's responsible for almost 50% of every dollar spent online in the US.[129] In the UK, 40% of adults have an Amazon Prime account.[130] Amazon ran for fourteen years in the red (showing losses)[131] and even though it has generated over $1 trillion in sales since 2005, and made $340 billion in gross profit over the same period, it managed to use tax laws to arrive at only $20 billion of taxable net income.[132] In fact, amazingly, Amazon received a $129 million tax rebate in 2018. I must add here, Amazon has done nothing illegal. It's our messed-up tax laws that enable Amazon and others to do this.

Sixty companies in the US Fortune 500 paid $0 tax in 2018, including GM, Prudential, Delta and many non-eco-friendly oil and gas companies, such as Halliburton and Chevron. That's just wrong.

The solution is easy, very easy. Tax *income*, not profit, like we do with people. This will remove all tax loopholes, and companies will pay tax in the country where they generate revenue. I would recommend a simple 25% corporate income tax rate on revenue. It would be similar in operation to personal income tax, and be applied instead of VAT, basically, a flat-rate tax on corporate income.

So, if a company earns money in a country, it is taxed in that country. No loopholes. Amazon, Google, Facebook etc. would pay tax where they earn income. If they are earning money from country X, then they should pay their fair share to country X for the ability to do so. If they don't, they can't sell their products and services in that country and instead, it will open an opportunity for a local entrepreneur.

Offshore IP (Intellectual Property) and Transfer Pricing

By taxing income, we would also be able to end the practice of transfer pricing. Transfer pricing is the term for companies 'buying' things from each other internally. Coupled with offshore tax shelters, this is one of the popular ways that companies use to get their money offshore.

A widely used method is to put the company's IP (Intellectual Property) offshore. How it works is pretty straightforward. The local company creates an offshore company in a zero or low tax jurisdiction. The local company then transfers the local company's IP to the offshore company. The offshore company then licenses the IP back to the local company. This is used widely, particularly for royalty payments (rock stars do this as well), software licensing, patents, trademarks, knowhow and franchise fees.

One example is Apple. When an iPhone is sold, say in the UK, the local company pays the offshore company for the IP. So, if the phone costs say £1,000 to purchase, they could pay £800 to their offshore company for the IP. Of course, this reduces their UK profits and thus their UK tax bill. That's how Apple have accrued almost $300 billion offshore. It's also how Starbucks paid $5.9 million in tax on $213 million of profit in the UK (2.8% tax rate) in 2017. In the fourteen years to 2012 Starbucks only paid £8.6 million in UK tax.[133] It charges itself for using its IP, the trademark 'Starbucks' and franchise fees.

Another method that companies use is to 'book' sales in a low tax jurisdiction. Google is a prime example of a company that was taking advantage of this. Its UK staff sold advertising to UK companies, but booked it in Ireland. Less profit to the UK, less tax to the UK, but that's where the business really was. Amazon does it through Luxembourg.

The best way to get around all this is to tax income, not profits.

The social tax system we've been discussing will help decrease much financial inequality, as some assets are slowly and fairly redistributed over time.

If you think about it, it's actually pretty simple and we're already essentially doing the income part by receiving a paycheck. So, what's stopping us doing it right now? What are the hurdles?

The rich. Some people at the top of the pyramid are not paying their fair share. They are legally skimming off all the cream or doing financial jiggery. The 10% of the 1% own the assets and they do not want to lose their reward system, because they are the beneficiaries.

I don't advocate just taking money away from the rich. That would cause a lot of problems globally, be unfair on some people, and not solve the environmental issues we face. As we've seen though, the easiest and best way to put things back in financial balance is through taxation and the removal of the complex rules that only the super-rich take advantage of.

Long Term Investing – Capital Gains Social

We should also use taxes to encourage long-term investment. While people may want to make a quick buck, the reality is, it takes time. We invest in businesses and they invest in R&D Research & Development) to create new products and services. Getting a return from investing takes time. We need to give businesses this time. Right now, we don't, and business leaders have responded accordingly. By law, companies have to look out for the interests of the shareholders. While that's fine, those interests have been deemed to be short-term returns, which benefit speculators, rather than long-term ones, which benefit us all. In the end, short-termism hurts everyone.

Many large companies these days are focused on profits and not innovation. 'Shareholder value' is the goal, not the betterment of the company by making more, and better. Remember, top management are heavily comprised of MBA's and bean counters. Product development is slow because the goal is to extract as much value out of the company as possible *this quarter*, not within five years. Cost cutting is more popular than R&D.

Vested interests don't want to pay the price of having to reinvent themselves. They've got a cash cow and they want it to remain that way and milk it for all it's worth. Some of these businesses are in oil, fracking, or plastic. Instead of being leaders and pushing into new ways of delivering eco-friendly services, packaging and goods, these companies want to hold onto what they have now.

Even technology companies suffer from this. If Kodak had had their way, we'd still be using film, even though they invented the first digital camera in 1975. They were up to 1.4mn pixels by 1986, but they refused to invest and wouldn't change. And that's why it all went tits up for Kodak. The writing was on the wall from when they created their original invention in 1975. Kodak could have owned this new space – a space they invented. Once the largest photography player in the world, Kodak filed for bankruptcy in 2012 and now doesn't exist as it once did – and ironically, all because of a focus on short-term profits and a lack of vision, from a company that had once been renowned for excellence in both.

Think about it, Kodak was put out of business by the very product they developed. And hey, they had a twenty-year head start on everyone. How insane is that?

Xerox, Hewlett Packard, Ford, GM (General Motors) and many other companies, who were once leaders in their fields, have killed their long-term prospects by focusing on quarterly returns. Focusing on money instead of value, their short sightedness eventually cost their shareholders as well. It's what almost killed cities such as Detroit, Cleveland and Pittsburgh and created the 'rust belt'. Xerox, not Apple, invented the computer interface we all know and use now. But blew it due to short termism.

Get this, the share price of Apple stock went down 25% the day they announced the launch of the iPod. Shouldn't it have gone up 25% that day? As Rana Foroohar, a renowned financial journalist, points out in her book 'Makers and Takers', most US companies have turned into financial companies, not product companies, and are staffed by MBA's focused on quarterly results, not product investment and growth.[134] Their growth is primarily driven by buying other companies, rather than creating new innovative products and services. The term 'Makers and Takers' is apt and gathering momentum to describe financiers who are taking the money – but not making anything of social value.

We need to tackle this short-termism, this quarterly reporting mentality.

Seems to me, the best way to tackle this is through taxes. Shareholders and investors should be rewarded for holding investments long term. This will end a lot of speculation, bring a great deal of stability to the markets, and motivate companies to invest in the future. The longer you hold a share, the less tax you pay when you sell it.

When you buy a share there are two ways to make money: the increase in share price (capital gains) and dividends (income).

Taxing dividends is pretty easy. Dividend income is part of your income. But, we need to stop companies being tempted to pay excess dividends in order to inflate share prices. This can be achieved through a CGT (Capital Gains Tax) on a graduated tax scale, starting at say five years, so that short-term share price gains are more heavily taxed.

CGT, the increase in share price, can be levied at different rates, depending on how long you've had the shares. The longer a share is held, the less CGT you pay on the profit you make. If you hold a share for five years or more, you pay the normal, 25% or 50% CGT, on the profit depending on your tax band. Hold a share for one day, it's 90% CGT tax on the profit. Hold shares for ten years and it's either 12.50% or 25% CGT (half the usual rate).

If a share loses money, then the loss portion is offset against other CGT gains. The tax revenue that comes in via capital gains tax should be split between Social Tax and the Sovereign Wealth Fund. Each gets half.

This will make it easier for companies to start investing in the future. It will be in their interest. Many companies today have become more focused on quarterly profits and paying shareholders, and thus increasing their share prices, than their products and services. They are slowly cannibalising their businesses. With shareholders, and staff, being rewarded for holding shares longer, companies will be more interested in investing in R&D, staff skills improvement, and long-term planning, instead of solely maximising short-term results. Everyone's interests will be better aligned, and better products and services will be developed. Everyone benefits.

Sovereign Wealth Fund (SWF)

Now that we've got business interested in the long term, let's give them a further push and collectively invest in the long term of the country by creating a Sovereign Wealth Fund. A sovereign wealth fund invests money on behalf of the country for the long term. It is for the country. A SWF (Sovereign Wealth Fund) can invest in the future. Norway has the largest one of these in the world as all its North Sea oil revenue went into it, none of it was spent; all of it was reinvested. It has over $1 trillion in it (about $200,000 per citizen).

And that doesn't include the separate Pension Fund the country has. It's one area where Thatcher messed up big time in the UK and squandered a massive once in a lifetime opportunity. All privatisations and North Sea oil should have gone into a UK sovereign wealth fund, instead of being spent to bribe voters to win elections. Imagine where the UK would be now? I digress. The benefits of a Sovereign Wealth Fund are massive.

The fund can invest in large and small businesses, large and small projects. The SWF can direct investment into areas that are good for the long-term evolution of the country.

Money that comes into the SWF should be kept away from the politicians. It belongs to the country, the people, not the government of the day. The government of the day can receive 50% of the return each year and the other 50% should be reinvested.

And no, politicians won't do the investing. Professional investors will do it, venture capitalists, and investment managers – with capped fees. Good salaries and reasonable bonuses can be paid based on the fund's performance over years. Not just one year, so they can gamble with no downside – and no mega million $ bonuses.

The investments can be split into different areas – including venture capital. Part invested in the local country (including through grassroots) and part invested globally. Investment funds should be created for each of the following sectors:

Medical
Education
Social

Science
Infrastructure – Energy, rails, roads, the environment, the Internet etc.
Growth – new businesses areas and entrepreneurship

Investment funds should specialise in investing in these sectors and in the future.

A Radical Idea – But

Yesterday, out of curiosity, I was playing with some numbers related to consumer debt and quantitative easing. This led me to wanting to see the maths behind having the super-rich pay off all the consumer debt of Americans and Brits. The numbers were compelling, but I dismissed the idea. I am a capitalist after all. But, I changed my mind after looking at quantitative easing a bit more. Here are the numbers:

As we noted previously, the US super-rich own almost $30 trillion in assets (excluding what's stashed offshore). Total US consumer debt is $4 trillion.[135] So, if we took, sorry, taxed the 1% of the population's wealthy, just once, on their assets at a rate of 15%, we could wipe out ALL consumer debt in the US. This would cause absolutely no hardship for the 30,000 people but would make 300 million people a lot happier and remove their major stress. Just sayin'.

Think about this for second, the richest 500 people in the world saw their wealth increase 25% in 2019, while the average person can't even earn 1 percent interest at the bank. The wealth of 500 people increased in one year by $1.2 trillion, the equivalent of one third of all the consumer and student debt in the US.

To put things really in perspective, look at this: total US household debt is $13 trillion,[136] meaning that those super-rich 1% could also pay off EVERY mortgage in the country, as well as ALL the consumer debt, including theirs, with a one-off 43% social tax and still be sitting on $17 trillion.

As I slept, or tried to, I couldn't stop thinking about these numbers. While the mortgage part was a bridge too far, I've come to the conclusion that having the 30,000 US rich pay off the US consumer debt of 300 million Americans is not just a good idea, but eminently fair. This is why:

- As we noted, the rich have been paying less tax. If they pay tax, it's 20%, whereas the kindergarten teacher is paying 25%. They've not been paying their fair share for a while now. This is just catch-up

- They'll be paying themselves. Think about it, who owns the debt? The super-rich do, as they own the companies that issued the debt

- $1.6 trillion of the debt is student debt and $1.1 trillion of that is owed to the US government. This would lower the US government debt and stop Betsy Devos, the US Secretary of Education, from selling it to her company,[137] where she would increase interest and cause yet further hardship for borrowers

- It prevents impending student loan defaults. Estimates are that by 2023, 40% of student loan borrowers may default – and millions suffer

- The wealthy caused the financial crash and then benefitted from it. They should pay for their speculation, not us

The UK tells a similar story. Total UK consumer debt is £428 billion and the richest 1% are worth £3 trillion (excluding all the money stashed offshore). If we levied a one-off wealth tax of 14% on the richest 1%, all consumer debt in the UK would be wiped out. Bearing in mind that this debt has doubled since the crash of 2008, a crash that was due to the super-rich financiers, it seems perfectly reasonable to me.

A number of very wealthy people in the US already agree with something similar. In June 2019, some of the richest people in the US wrote an open letter to all the 2020 US Presidential candidates[138] calling for a yearly wealth tax, such as that proposed by Elizabeth Warren, of 2% on assets over $50 million, and another 1% on assets over $1 billion. They reckoned it would generate $1 trillion in new taxes over a period of ten years. Signatories include Disney heiress, Abigail Disney, Facebook co-founder, Chris Hughes, investor, George Soros, and Blue Haven Initiative co-founders, Liesel Pritzker Simmons and Ian Simmons.[139]

Star Trek Or Blade Runner

As we enter the 2020's the world as we know it is changing and we will not recognise today in twenty years. What's next – and who's going to choose? We must evolve.

We are at a crossroads and have some important choices to make. But we seem to be sleepwalking into them. No one appears to be addressing the overall fundamental, big-picture issues to offer solutions. In a nutshell, the choice is simple. Do we want a Blade Runner future or a Star Trek future?

If we want a Blade Runner future, it's likely that if we continue to trundle along as we are now, we'll simply stumble into it. If we want a Star Trek future, we need to think out of the box, big time. You see, what is fundamentally changing is humans – us, because of technology. We're putting ourselves out of a job. The human race is making itself redundant, obsolete. Technology is doing what *we* used to do. It's enhanced our lives both at home and in the workplace, from initially making simple tasks easier (hammer and screwdriver), to doing mundane and routine automated tasks more efficiently (assembly lines), to now doing complicated tasks (robotics and self-driving cars). And watch as AI (Artificial Intelligence) and machine automation creep further and further up the food chain into all facets of our lives. Twenty years from now we will not recognise the lives we live today.

A Blade Runner future would see a small group of people at the top of the food chain owning almost everything and their lieutenants controlling our lives. It would be a world where most people would be living, if you can call it that, in a wrecked and unsafe natural environment. Surviving day-to-day, waiting for the planet's extinction. It's a grim thought.

Or we can aspire to a Star Trek future and seek to create a world where everyone's needs are met, the natural environment respected and appreciated, and where we work together globally to evolve humankind to the next level; a world where technology works for everyone and coexists to everyone's benefit. In a Star Trek future, we could work together to do big things – like embrace the environment and search the stars.

The question is how do we make it so?

This won't happen by magic and it will take some serious soul searching. We need to question ourselves and collectively decide what the new purpose of humankind is. The choice is still ours.

Our prime motivation to this point has been largely centred around bettering our own lives. Whatever your political views, there is no arguing that personal self-interest, when coupled with a motivated and focused group, has resulted in a massive increase in everyone's quality of life, particularly in Level 3 and 4 countries.

There is no question that basic life, quality of food, shelter and clothing, for the average person now are far better than even the wealthy of even a hundred years ago. But, we have a predicament. The automation that can remove all our primary needs and improve our lives is also making us obsolete. The rewards are going to the few, the environment is being abused and people are suffering. What to do?

Even if we can sort out the financial inequality, what is our value?

Actually, for most people it's quantified already. Most receive a paycheck, and consumer spending is responsible for over 70% of the US and UK economies.

That being the case, let's protect people, not jobs, with UI (Universal Income). Combined with environmental credits and debits, UH (Universal Healthcare) and UE (Universal Education), let's see what the world could look like.

Universal Income (UI)

Before getting into the nitty-gritty of this, let's take a quick look at the economy: we know that consumer spending accounts for about 70% of it and that almost year-on-year, since the 50's, the share of the economy driven by consumer spending has continued to increase.

So, that means people spending money is the best way to help the economy.

By spending, people create demand for goods and services. This creates jobs and raises more taxes for the government. Makes sense.

If people have money, they spend it. That being the case, it would seem logical to find a way to make sure people have enough money to spend.

Trickle-down doesn't work. The cock-eyed theory that if the rich pay less in tax they will spend and invest more doesn't happen in real life.

But trickle-*up* will work. Give the average person $1,000 and they spend it on goods and services. It trickles up. It helps the economy and the community. Give a wealthy person $1,000 and it makes no difference on their spending.

Universal Income (UI) is not a new idea. In fact, it's been tested in a number of places[140] with outstanding results. Alaska created its own Sovereign Wealth Fund and since 1982 has been paying residents a UI. In 2015, a family of four in Alaska would have received $8,288.[141] US democratic candidate Andrew Yang wants to give all Americans $1,000 a month.[142] And there are many places trying it out around the world,[143] including the US. Sadly, Ontario just cancelled a popular three-year experiment that started in 2017 but stopped after two years due to its new right-wing government.[144] It was an experiment that was going well and had positive effects on people and the local community. People ate better, health improved, people helped local charities and even helped to keep museums open that would have had to close, if not for their 'free' work.[145]

We need to simplify things. We know we can pay everyone a UI. So, what would be the benefits? For starters, not just would it significantly reduce stress, but it would actually SAVE money.

In the UK, welfare currently accounts for more than half the income of 4.3 million families and cost £112 billion in 2017.[146] If each family is roughly four people, it means 8.6 million adults and 8.6 million children (a total of 17.2 million people), rely on welfare. That's 26% of the entire UK population.

Cost wise, that's £12,900 per adult. So why not give every adult a UI income of £12K per year? No hassles, no stress, and loads of people get to do more productive things with their time. This also happens to be the amount people can earn currently before they are taxed. We can get rid of the expensive bureaucracy that supports welfare as well as reduce the hassle and stress associated with getting it. And we're already spending the money anyway – but in an extremely inefficient way.

People would be able to work and not worry about losing their 'benefits'. This is a common problem welfare recipients face. If they earn money, they lose their benefits which means that they must have secure full-time jobs that will pay more than their benefits. They can't do part-time or short-term work. The existing system currently forces them to remain on benefits.

With UI, they can earn more money, help the economy and pay tax with no fear of going hungry or homeless – and with a hell of a lot less stress.

Then, there are pensions, on which the UK spends £156 billion annually. There are 5.3 million pensioner families.[147] If half these families are made up of two people, that equates to 7.95 million people. That's 12% of the total UK population. Cost wise, that's £19,622 per person (multiply this x 2 for couples).

26% welfare + 12% pensions = 38%

This means that 38% of the population are already essentially receiving UI! But, it's in a very convoluted way that is expensive to run, demoralising and stressful for most.

Remember, this is forest, not trees. Think about the concept, not the transitioning. There are others who can do a far better job at it than me. But, I believe UI is eminently doable and should be done. Now.

What about everyone else? By coincidence, they are already receiving a UI. It's the £12,000 tax-free allowance.

To keep things simple, everyone needs to receive the same UI. Everyone. On the day of the month they were born would be practical. While some people may not work as well, they will still be contributing to the economy by spending their UI and I really can't see the bulk of the adult population stopping working because of a UI of £12K. Who's going to give up a £20K, £50K or £100K salary and that lifestyle for 12K?

With UI, every adult receives £1,000 monthly from the government. Everyone can work and earn as much as they want, and it has no impact on their UI. The UI is not taxed. When they work, they contribute 25% of their earnings to Social Tax. If someone were earning £100K, they would contribute 25% of the £100K (£25K) in Social Tax.

UI also makes dealing with the declining population easier as raising children now is quite expensive. Whether losing one person's income to stay at home or paying for day-care, it takes money to raise and support children. Let's make it easier to have children and raise them, not harder as it is now. They are our most important assets and our future.

The guardian of the child, until age eighteen, can receive another 50% of UI or £500 in this case. There is always a maximum allowance of two children (we need 2.1 to maintain our population). If the population is dropping, the number of children the guardian can receive UI for, can be increased temporarily to say three.

If we gave every adult in the country a UI of £12,000 per year it would cost us less than we spend now. Look at the benefits: every child and adult would have a floor, a basic minimum living standard. The angst of bureaucracy navigation or the stress of putting food on the table would be eliminated for 9.6 million people. Kids wouldn't go hungry. No one would need to live on the streets. Crime would drop. Think about it. Think about people you know, friends, family and those you interact with daily. What kind of an impact would it have on them psychologically – and on you? You can almost hear the giant national (global) exhale of stress. It's wonderful.

Let's also not forget the entrepreneurial spirit that UI would help foster. If people, especially those with fewer family resources to fall back on, had a minimum floor, they would be more tempted to try new things and start new businesses. Whether a new organic fruit café, a new app, or painting, or music, people would be able to pursue their creative dreams without as much worry of 'failure'.

In ten years, we'll look back to pre-UI days and shudder. Stress, people going hungry, living on the streets, crime, more stress, and we'll wonder why we had so much stress in society when much of it could be removed so easily with UI. Britain will be a much happier nation. Even if someone is 'homeless' they will, with dignity, be able to afford a room in a 'homeless' shelter. And what they'll pay the shelter will enable it to provide a good and compassionate service to them.

It's all do-able! What are we waiting for?

Did I mention prisons? Why do many people offend and reoffend? It's because they need money. When they leave prison, they have no money and no job. It costs £37,000 to keep someone in prison for a year in the UK.[148] £12K is a lot less, plus it has other benefits like socialisation and opportunity. They'd have money to spend on what *they* want. No need to steal. Of course, I'm not an idiot, I don't think for a moment that this will stop crime entirely, but it can certainly be argued that it'll reduce it.

UI also puts a minimum value on each person's time. If the time is spent doing nothing more than buying things to live, people are still contributing to the economy and the overall health of society. If they have a child, the child brings with them another £500 of value. A parent can then either stay home and take care of the child or spend the money on day-care while they go to work. The choice is theirs, but either way the paid babysitter vs. day-care being part of GDP, is addressed.

UI would also mean that children wouldn't go hungry at school or be shamed for not being able to afford lunch. 30% of UK children live below the poverty line.[149] In the US it's 20%.

What kind of a world do we live in where a school will embarrass a five or fifteen-year-old about owing lunch money and make them go hungry – while watching others eat? This is torture and morally wrong.

I don't think most of us want to live in a world where children go hungry and where a nine-year-old, Ryan Kyote in California, puts us to shame. Ryan was already using his lunch card to pay for lunches at his elementary school when he heard that a five-year-old in Indiana was denied lunch. Ryan turned around and paid off the entire $74.80 lunch debt of his third-grade class by using the pocket money he had saved up over six months.[150] What a wonderful person! We need our society to be that kind. Ryan knows what's right and sees it. Why can't we? Most of us can.

While the Chobani founder, Hamdi Ulukaya gallantly stepped up to the plate and paid off the entire amount of the lunch debt of his Rhode Island

School district.[151] He shouldn't have had to. He wouldn't have needed to if all the super-rich had paid their fair share.

Universal Healthcare (UH)

One of the biggest things to impact our lives is our health. It's actually the most important component. If our physical or mental being is not good, neither are we. We, and those around us suffer, society suffers, and we lose our sense of value. It undermines us. When a person is in need of health care, we shouldn't compound things by adding the second major stress, money. That just makes a bad problem worse.

The UK has its NHS and although it has its problems, we are immensely proud of it and we take great comfort from knowing that should we need health services, they will be there for us. We're covered. It's a major stress point removed.

If we imagine someone becoming ill in the US, our first thought is, are they insured? If they aren't, we know they're about to go through hell. They will go without treatment and often become bankrupt. If you're uninsured in the US, you worry about this a lot. You're terrified. Now imagine how people would feel if they had the NHS behind them. You can feel the stress relief.

People recover faster and better with less stress, and for the Republicans out there, that means people are healthier and more productive workers.

The NHS is envied by much of the world. Yet, people are trying to dismantle it through stealth, so they can make more money from it. This should be stopped.

The NHS and social services do need a rethink as many social services have been thrown into the NHS' remit. The population is aging, and the NHS is being stretched. What people need from healthcare has changed so we need to retool the NHS for tomorrow, not dismantle it for the financiers.

The irony regarding UH in the UK is that many people don't realise the Conservatives are slowly dismantling the NHS and sending it down the path of privatisation, including letting American healthcare and pharma companies in as part of a post Brexit deal with the US. (Simultaneously, Americans are, for the first time, really beginning to clamour more and more for their own NHS. Most Democratic contenders for the 2020 election are calling for it).

And certainly, the NHS is being dismantled by the government of the day. Don't kid yourself. We must work hard to protect Universal Healthcare. Otherwise, we will end up with a US style one – which the BMA (British Medical Association) believes is the government's intent.[152]

The NHS removed this health stress from us as a nation by taking away that terrifying worry of the costs and stresses of becoming ill - and now we can't imagine life without it. The same will be true of UI and UH. Combined, we will have a healthier and happier society. And future generations will wonder how we ever lived without them.

It's obvious. Universal Healthcare is a must. It's necessary for our physical and mental wellbeing.

A couple of small changes though, could very rapidly improve the service the hard-working doctors and nurses strive to provide. A more efficient system, that provides access to pharmacists and practical nurses for consultation on minor ailments or complaints could be set up. This together with a nominal fee for GP visits would reduce the logjam for GP appointments. In addition, a small fee for tests and a minor prescription charge would help offset the steep costs these incur and avoid wastage.

Care for the elderly needs a complete rethink. It's as much social as it is medical. Let's bring the NHS into the 21st century. As for the US, it needs an NHS and there are many people there who ardently believe in Universal Healthcare. No question about it.

Universal Education (UE)

After getting rid of student debt, let's not bring it back. It's a scam for the rich anyway. In the UK, student loans were initiated by the Labour government – which is ironic. Rather than being interest-free or charging interest at the rate the government can borrow money (currently less than 0.5 %), the loans' interest rate was instead set at the RPI (Retail Price Index) – the rate of inflation. Okay. But then, in 2012 the government sold the loans to private companies who now charge RPI plus 3%, plus more, depending on your salary. In other words, the government could have borrowed the money at less than 1% and charged students that. But instead, if a student is earning £40,000, they pay 7% interest.

While originally the loans didn't accrue interest until students left university, now they accrue immediately. Remember those loan charts and think about this. The amount the student owes is actually going up each month while they're at university and once they leave, even if they make the minimum legal payment, their debt continues to rise. Expectations in the UK are that only 17% of students will repay their loans in full and after thirty years, while 47% of the loans will be written off – which actually means paid off by the taxpayers.[153] And why doesn't anyone mind that the loans won't be repaid? Just remember those interest graphs, that's because the students' debt grows, and students will actually pay back far more in interest than they borrowed in the first place. They will have paid off the principal (the amount they borrowed) numerous times by the time the loan is written off. It's a cash cow for the super-rich. One subsidised by the taxpayer yet again.

If, however, we give UI to everyone over eighteen, students wouldn't need to borrow the money to go into higher education – they'd be able to pay for it. And the government wouldn't have to pay either. UI is a winner.

I find it interesting that just as the UK begins charging students for education, in the US most Democrats are now making calls to write off all student debt and to stop charging for education. The debt is crippling the middle classes in the US. We can already see this debt having a crippling effect in the UK. We need to stop charging for education in the UK and the US – and we need to bring back polytechnics in the UK. Polytechnics tend to be focused on more vocational training such as nursing, teaching, engineering and the arts, and courses can be different lengths, compared to university courses, which are more academic (literature, chemistry, politics). While there is no firm divider, the concept of having flexible further education is needed to deal with the immense amount of retraining that will soon be required, as well as the new learning we'll need as we live longer and switch careers more often.

As an aside, writing off the existing student debt by taxing the super-rich is something some wealthy, enlightened philanthropists are doing of their own volition. Billionaire, Robert Smith was giving the commencement speech at his alma mater, Morehouse College, when he surprised everyone by telling them he was paying off all their student loans – all four hundred of them![154] I'm sure that put a smile on a few faces.

Pensions

We're living longer. Society and jobs are changing. Our interests are evolving. It's time to phase out pensions, as we know them currently. We should all have a personal pension, a tax-free Life Saving Plan, one we can dip in and out of throughout our lives. If we had UI this would be far easier as everyone would essentially have a basic pension, so no one would go hungry. Coupled with a Life Saving Account, no pun intended, we would be more able to change careers, retrain, broaden our minds or just take a breather.

How would this work in practice? Let's keep it simple. Each year you could deposit up to three times UI into a Life Saving account (that would be £36,000 in our example). Income (dividends and CGT) earned on that money would be tax free, as long as it remained in the account. If it was drawn down, that draw down would be taxed as income at 25% at source. People would be fairly passive investors and put their money index tracker funds (indexes are grouped of companies – like the stock markets). Let's be realistic, most people don't have the knowledge or patience to be successful active investors.

When our time comes, our Life Saving Plan becomes part of our estate for inheritance tax purposes. Now, let's make sure we leave behind an environment that our grandchildren can live in.

The Green Revolution

It's clear. We need a Green Revolution - one that all of society is focused on. And it's vitally important that we do it now if we want to protect our children and humanity.

Today, a private individual or a company can buy a piece of land. Yet, there's no cost to them for what they do with the land. They are not charged for the environmental toll on their use of that land. If they chop down the trees for firewood or to make things, or they extract coal or gold or other minerals, there's no associated environmental fee for the value being extracted.

There needs to be a system of eco-debits and eco-credits. For instance, if you chop a tree down, it's an eco-debit. If you plant another tree, it's an eco-credit. If you take minerals out of the ground, it's an eco- debit, and so on.

Investment in the environment needs to be a priority. As does slowing and reversing the destruction we've been doing. We can do it and we must do it. This is an area where government and Sovereign Wealth Funds can really help out. Both of them can direct funds into good environmental activities. Ideas abound and eco businesses are being created to develop and deploy new environmentally friendly solutions. This is great for the environment and stimulates massive job creation. This is the Green Revolution.

There is actually loads of amazing tech being deployed and developed for alternative renewable energy at the moment. We need to invest more in these areas and simultaneously tax fossil fuels heavily with the environmental eco-debits. This will create whole new businesses focused around renewable energy. Even in China, solar and renewable are getting traction. Three-hundred-and-forty-four Chinese cities have lower solar energy prices than their coal grid and the country is investing $367 billion in renewables.[155] China I also beginning to tackle plastic and has banned the use of all non-degradable bags (not just shopping bags) by the end of 2020.[156] Do we want to be left behind? Can we afford to be?

We need to value the environment more and include environmental costs in all products and services, a system of debits and credits. Carbon tax credits don't begin to go far enough. And yes, there are some glaring 'quick fixes' we can do right now. Eat half as much beef for starters. As the recent IPCC (Intergovernmental Panel on Climate Change) points out, we've already damaged a quarter of the ice-free land on earth and negatively impact 70% of it. Livestock contribute 14.5% of that.[157] We can, and should, use our wallets and voting power to push for change. We have the power. Don't buy what's not right and don't vote for what's wrong.

Time to dispose of our disposable society. We need to make things that last; things that don't have built-in obsolescence (the practice of making things that we know will break at a certain time). Phones and computers for instance. Why can't we swap old parts out instead of throwing them away? Why aren't these products modules? (Because they make the manufacturers more money this way.) We should make things repairable, recyclable and expandable. Thankfully, the first steps are being taken. From the beginning of 2020, there's a new EU 'right to repair' law that impacts white goods – washing machines, dishwashers, fridges, TV's – and will be expanded in future to include other items[158]. The new law will have numerous benefits, including reducing CO_2 emissions and landfills, as well as saving people hundreds of Euros each year.

We can remove subsidies that are hurting the environment and use them to help the environment. In the UK alone, airlines don't pay fuel duty and there is no VAT on ticket sales, industry savings of £10 billion a year, while rail only gets £4 billion in subsidies. Why don't we remove the breaks to the airlines, apply it to the rail network, and run the rail network more efficiently, as they do in the rest of Europe?

Globally, coal, oil and gas receive over $370 billion in subsidies, compared to $100 billion for renewables. What's really amazing about this is that clean renewables are actually generating more jobs than fossil fuel. In California there are five times more clean energy jobs than fossil fuel jobs.[159] Let's cancel the fossil fuel subsidies and plough that money into investing in our future – in renewables.[160] There's solar, wind, wave, hydrogen and so many promising opportunities. We just need to back them properly.

We should also look more closely at natural nutrients in the soil. Using biodegradable food waste for instance, doesn't just enrich the soil – it also sucks CO_2 out of the atmosphere. And yes, it sounds simple: let's plant loads more trees.

Years ago, people started talking about a Green Deal and it's really come to everyone's attention with Alexandria Ocasio-Cortez in the US calling for a Green New Deal – a play on Roosevelt's New Deal for getting out of the Great Depression. Which is interesting, as we also need a Green Revolution to help offset job losses, due to the end of the automobile revolution. A Green Revolution makes sense. There are some very clever and informed people out there who see this, but time is of the essence.

We need to do this now!

And capitalism is not dead – we just need to make the invisible hand visible. There are whole new industries that can sprout up around the environment and social enterprises. New products and services can be created that will result in new jobs. Whether it's venetian blinds that double as solar panels that need designing, installing and maintaining; hemp production; taking care of nature, or finding new technology, such as graphene[161] and borophene,[162] there will be many new jobs created to support these new eco solutions. And there's space exploration of course. There are some truly exciting opportunities ahead of us. Let's get on with making them happen.

The People Revolution

Where else do we need people? Social orientated jobs for starters: teaching, health care, social care, community care, environmental care. These jobs are much needed, yet organisations find it difficult to recruit and keep people, as salaries are too low and the jobs very demanding. This will change with UI and new tax policies.

There are huge demands for people in the social caring arena – taking care of children, older people and others who need assistance, to name a few – even vanilla companionship. Being lonely is unhealthy for us and being with people is better for us than exercise.[163] Loneliness is particularly prevalent with older people. In fact, research points to the effect of loneliness as the equivalent of smoking 15 cigarettes a day.[164]

We certainly don't want this. People are compassionate. It hurts us to see others suffering. We naturally want to help. So, let's evolve to a system that puts value on helping, and rewards the helpers. Not one that solely rewards production.

Likewise, due to UI and taxes, the arts would flourish. People would have the time and resources to spend following their passions – and they wouldn't need to be rock stars or famous to make a living at it. Want to work part time and paint or be in a band? No problem. Want to make a film? Or open a gallery? You could.

And what about gap years, career changes and education? We're all living a lot longer and the whole concept of retirement has to change. It's a bit much to expect that the profession someone chose at eighteen or twenty-two is something they will want to do for fifty, sixty or seventy years, non-stop. As we get older, we'll want to do different things. Physically we simply won't be able to do some jobs, but mentally, we'll have changed as well. We'll need to take gap years: to retool, travel, and learn, for fun and/or to train for different professions.

The healthiest and most satisfied retired people are those that remain active - whether helping local charities, learning or assisting new businesses. Let's make it easy for people to do this and keep contributing and adding value to society. Give people the breathing space to do volunteer work.

We are about to have an avalanche of people looking for jobs. The end of the automobile revolution is literally minutes away. We're in the winding down stage. In April 2019, Elon Musk, the founder of Tesla cars, announced that he expects to have one million *robotaxis* on the road in 2020.[165] That's one million self-driving cars. Even if it takes him an extra year or two, the automobile revolution is over.

And as for those naysayers that claim people won't trust self-driving cars and say it won't happen, they're wrong. I love driving and like many people my age have an inherent distrust of a self-driving car. But that is irrelevant. I'll have to get used to it. People felt that way about the horseless carriage (automobile) when it first came out. Well, now it's a driverless carriage. All of us would do well to get with the program and as a society we need to prepare for it - NOW. The good news is that this means there are lots of people to fill the new roles we'll be creating and because of UI, UE and UH. The transition doesn't have to be painful.

We could also learn a few things from countries such as Denmark. McDonalds employees there make a minimum wage of $20/hour. McDonalds is making plenty of money. Yet there's no actual minimum wage in Denmark. The staff and the employers worked together to agree the minimum wage. They can do this because Denmark protects workers, not jobs.[166] This is what UI, UE and UH can do. They protect workers so you don't need to protect jobs.

As Marc Sabatier Hvidkjaer points out, while two thirds of Danes belong to unions, McDonalds could fire staff if they need to, and there would be no strikes or huge redundancy pay-outs. This is because of 'The Danish Model', whose roots go back to 1899. In a nutshell, employers recognised that employees were allowed to organise into unions while employees recognised that employers could lead and distribute labour, as they needed. These groups work together and compromise.[167]

For the hard-core capitalists who want flexible hiring, this is another good reason to have UI, UE and UH. They mean you don't need have to have such strong government regulations around hiring and firing, as many socialist countries have. In countries such as France and Portugal, businesses are reluctant to hire staff, as they can't get rid of them if the business has problems. With UI, these stringent rules could be relaxed so that in downturns it would be easier for a company to make layoffs and in good times, more tempting for the company to hire quickly. Interestingly, that would likely minimise some of the economic swings we have now, as it would be easier to make little tweaks in hiring to meet demand, up and down, before things become desperate and a company hires or fires many people in one go.

Tied in with this, members of staff need representation on company decision-making, not just for pay, but for the products and services the company provides. Staff on the front line would naturally be better placed to see things that management don't. It could be anything from little changes to improve production, to removing something that customers always have difficulty with – or coming up with the next great product.

The taxation and incentives proposed above would balance an awful lot out within twenty years. It would start the pendulum that has swung in one direction since the 80's, to swing back in the other direction and minimise further crashes.

Personal Data and Privacy

Our personal data has to be looked at as well. Today, data harvesting is big business. Many of the biggest companies in the world are watching us, collecting data on us and making money from it. We have become the product – and we're not being paid for it.

Google, Amazon and Facebook are three huge examples. They make a fortune from our data, from watching us – and don't pay us, or even our governments, much tax. Even the local supermarket knows more about us than we do.

And the young don't appreciate the value of their privacy.

If we have to pay to watch a video that someone has created, which is quite right, then companies should pay to watch us. And we should be in control of our data. Deciding who can use our personal data, where, how and for how long. We need in on this game.

I just discovered that while Google decided to stop reading our emails to target advertising at us, instead Google now reads our emails to grab our purchase history, otherwise known as receipts.[168] Google of course have it in their T&C's and say that they're providing a service – one they decided to bury in Settings - Accounts - Payments - and Subscriptions. Hmm, I wonder if they're more interested in learning our spending habits to target ads and searches at us – plus God only knows what else? Eventually, they'll know everything about us. No more mystery, just another contender for our digital identity so they can sell our data and target us. All the big boys are doing it one way or another. Apple Card for instance, married with all other Apple services. Yet another digital identity contender – and the list goes on.

Content (whether posts, advertising or new articles) is targeted at us based on our previous activity and location. Of course, the more we see and read this content, the more targeted content we see. The platforms aiming this content at us claim they are doing us a favour by giving us what we want. The reality though is that this content and these platforms are making us more narrow-minded. We only see what reinforces our currently held views, beliefs and interests. We never hear the other side of the argument and think, 'Hmm, they may have a point'. They stifle debate and exploration. They hinder us developing new interests and knowledge. Personally, I have changed my mind and views on many things. Through my life I have developed new pursuits and interests. I have learned and discovered new things by stumbling across articles that I read, simply because the headline attracted my attention. I'm sure many of us do this. Humans are naturally curious, but content targeted too precisely removes new things that may stimulate our curiosity.

The magnitude of the manipulation of our personal data is not trifling. Did I mention AWS (Amazon Web Services)? Most people will likely not have heard of it but it's part of the backbone of the Internet and brought in over half of Amazon's revenues in 2018.[169] AWS is the technical infrastructure used by many cloud Internet services, over 34% of them.

Microsoft, Google and IBM have 11%, 8% and 6% respectively.[170] These are also the companies trying to manage and sell us - and our identities. We are their products...

...Which dovetails into privacy. We should be able to opt out. Why is the UK the most watched nation in the world?[171] Are its citizens really that bad that we need facial recognition tracking our every move? The security stuff is a lie. However, China is about to overtake the UK as the most watched nation and have already gone further with their implementation. Even now, it's using facial recognition to monitor and control its citizens by issuing a social credit score that can stop you boarding trains. You jaywalk, your score goes down and you receive a text message with a fine.[172] China announced that (from Dec 1, 2019), you'd need to pass a facial recognition test in order to buy a smartphone.[173] It's all Black Mirror and it's happening today.

The good news: the EU is considering giving people explicit rights over the use of their facial recognition data to stop it being used indiscriminately.[174]

Most of us aren't saints. We sometimes break little rules. It's fun. Really, do we want to kill this? I'm sure we all have fond memories of breaking these decrees, sneaking into that swimming pool or club or skinny-dipping after hours. These experiences actually helped make us what we are. This is freedom.

But governments and companies are taking this freedom away. In Sweden they're now even chipping people to ride the train.[175] Think about this for a minute. Are you shuddering yet?

And it's not only our personal freedom at stake. Watching us too closely also stifles creativity. Inventors and entrepreneurs are by definition rule breakers after all, and the loss of creativity is perhaps the most damaging aspect of the loss of privacy. We just need to take a look at the major breakthroughs we've gained from mistakes. Loads of inventions came about by accident. Watching us too closely will prompt us to try and hide our mistakes – instead of running with them.

Penicillin is a good example. Things went bad in an experiment Alexander Fleming was doing in 1928. He was looking into the flu and went on holiday for a couple of weeks and didn't seal a culture plate properly. When he returned, he found the damaged culture plate had something (penicillin) growing in it that was in turn stopping the growth of staphylococcus. Had he lived in a world the way China (and the rest of us) is heading, he would have tried to throw the plate away to hide the fact he hadn't sealed it properly, or he may have come back to find the thought-police there and his social credits docked.

Encryption is key to security and there is heated debate about it at the moment. The UK and the US want a backdoor into all our communications. Forgetting the obvious, innocent until proven guilty, it's basic spying.

If I can send a letter without the government reading it, why can't I do the same with a text message or email? And it's not practical – but governments simply don't understand the tech.

To begin with, the bad guys will always be able to use 'unbreakable' encryption. Not just is encryption already widely available and the norm now, but if – and that's a big 'if' – a government managed to break the existing coding, someone would update the encryption, so it was unbreakable again. It need not be a criminal organisation. It would likely be a privacy advocate and the code would be open source, so it could be checked and improved. Phil Zimmerman did this when he developed and released PGP (Pretty Good Privacy) in 1991.[176] The US government actually took Zimmerman to court in 1993 for 'munitions' export, as they said that legally the US and Americans were the only ones allowed to have it. This is because the government couldn't break the encryption. Zimmerman challenged this and released the source code. And, as it's code, which governments seem to have difficulty getting their heads around, it can be all over the world in milliseconds and used by anyone. They can't control it.

And now there's OpenPGP for everyone. Thank you Phil.

This brings up another point. Governments want a 'backdoor' into our communications. Who's to decide who can use this backdoor and how you control access? What if the government was Hitler or Stalin - or Trump? Or how about a staff member of the US NSA (National Security Agency), or a spy? You can't trust every single person who has access to it, nor even keep the backdoor access safe. The tools to access the backdoor can be stolen by criminals. On October 3, 2019 the top cops in the US, the UK and Australia wrote an open letter to Facebook asking Mark Zuckerberg not to enable end-to-end encryption on its messaging products which would have given governments a backdoor.[177] Thankfully the answer was 'no' to their snooping. But they won't stop trying

Let's look at what a backdoor is. Some people hide a key to their house outside, in case they lose their keys. Sometimes, it's a key to their backdoor. Don't put it under a flowerpot, that's the first place burglars check. Anyway, let's say all of us were required by law to keep a backdoor key hidden, wherever we like, but we had to tell the 'authorities' the location of this backdoor key. A few things would likely happen:

1. If someone hacked into the authority and accessed the database containing the locations of all our backdoor keys, everyone would be at risk. And we wouldn't necessarily know that someone had access to it. In the case of encryption, this risk is doubled as the company offering the service would also have a copy of the backdoor encryption key and that could be broken into.
2. Someone could have a friend in the authority or company and ask them for it. Or they could bribe them for it. Or they could blackmail them for it.
3. Someone in the authority or company could have a gripe with someone else – maybe an ex-spouse or boyfriend or girlfriend or colleague – and give themselves access to snoop. Or just enjoy snooping.
4. Politicians and dictators. Imagine what Trump could do if he could access his opponent's correspondence...
5. Corporate espionage. Yup, some companies would pay silly money for access to private correspondence.
6. If everyone had to have a backdoor key, burglars would look for them. It would only be a question of when they finally found the key, not if.

How real is the chance of being broken into? Happens all the time.

In 2016 the US NSA (National Security Agency), arguably the biggest spy agency in the world with the most resources, got broken into and a toolkit was stolen by, yup, hackers, a group called Shadow Brokers who then sold it on. And the tools were used to target cities, states, countries and companies, railroads and even the NHS.[178] These tools were used to create WannaCry and NotPetya[179] – the ransomware that encrypted people's hard drives and forced them to pay Bitcoin ransoms. In May 2017 hundreds of thousands of computers around the world were taken control of by a group of North Koreans demanding ransom. The NHS in the UK was crippled.[180]

On January 9, 2020 Amazon fired some staff that were spying on people who had purchased Amazon Ring home security from Amazon. Some security - when you can't even trust the company you bought it from, that manages it as well! [181]

Included were other tools that allowed the NSA to hack iPhones and Android devices. As well as accessing your data, these tools allow people to take pictures and listen to what you're saying.[182] And they can do this through your TV as well.[183]

If this all sounds a bit Big Brotherish – that's because it is!

The reality is that these tools are used against innocents by governments and bad guys. They don't catch bad guys, criminals and terrorists, who are always one step ahead. The best way to protect citizens is to make technology safe for everyone, by using technologies such as unbreakable encryption for all correspondence and data, and having a decentralised Internet.

You know those microchips the Swedes are using (similar to the ones in pets) or the biometric chips in your passport? These chips cost pennies and hackers can copy them. You say, 'But I wasn't there' and the cops say, 'But your chip says you were'. Same thing with facial recognition: your face can be 3D printed, so the authorities say, 'But we saw you there...' and the crooks and rulers of the day have all our information, our identity. And the bad guys are still out there, getting away with being bad.

As Joseph Heller famously said in Catch-22, 'Just because you're paranoid doesn't mean they aren't after you.'

Kids

Parents are heard to complain that kids and young adults today don't have the motivation of their own generation. Maybe, but parents and society helped created this situation. The young adults of today are how they are because of us. They are not to blame. No one is, and everyone is. We've all created the current situation we find ourselves in. Let's deal with it and quit pointing fingers.

Most people over about thirty-five still have the old values, the old purposes and the concept of 'an honest day's work for an honest day's pay'. But those under thirty-five grew up not needing to produce. Forget twenty-five-year-olds for a minute though and imagine today's two-year-olds in twenty years. They'll grow up in such a completely different world from the one we have now. They will think completely differently. Their values will be different. It's just a fact. You know it and we don't need $10 million spent on research to confirm it. Look around as you walk down the street. How many people are on their smart phones? Look at the toddler in her buggy with a tablet. Humankind is venturing into new territory.

Those over thirty-five had the luxury of boredom. Boredom is the most under-rated luxury we have. When we're bored, we get creative. Our minds wander. We dream. We imagine. We play. We do. But, we have this misguided notion that we must fill up all our time with activities. Increasingly, what used to be regarded as 'bored' time is now focused on our screens. That two-year-old in her stroller is so focused on her tablet that she's completely missing the world around her. She's not aware. She's not actually being positively stimulated, she's watching, not creating. She's not seeing a five-year-old with wings and wondering how fast they can fly. She's not wondering why the lights turn green or wondering how that cyclist stays on the bike as they pop a wheelie. She's not imagining herself doing that, nor is she laughing when a car sprays a puddle on a pedestrian. She's missing life. And it's getting worse.

In various countries around the world, it's being recognised that the magic of youth needs to be kept alive and fostered. In Finland they don't start 'school' as we think of it, at five, they wait till seven. Before this age, 'school' is about what four, five and six-year-olds really want to do, which is explore; learn by playing. They should be building forts, painting, laughing, making mud pies and singing. They should explore the environment around them. Let's let kids be kids. Let them get muddy and scraped up. They should 'learn' about the analogue world by being in the analogue world. Kids *should* get dirty and make forts and mud pies – already proven to be the best defence against all the allergies kids are having these days. And this should continue throughout their school lives.

In France they have banned mobile phones from schools until the age of fifteen. Hurrah! That's a great idea. Kids need to see screens and technology as tools that enhance their lives, not as their entire life. Sure, use tech at school and at home, but keep the 'social' at bay during school hours.

It's a start, but we still need to do more.

Social Service

Social service would be a good idea. No matter who you are you should do it, rich or poor, after turning eighteen, after you've finished high school, if you don't go straight into further education, and after FE (Further Education). One full year of social service, doing community related things, which includes: the environment, living and working with others, doing things that make us feel valuable, and that are valuable to society.

And every five years afterwards we should all return for a month and do it again. Get back in touch with our roots and society as a whole.

Politics And Politicians

Politics needs a complete rethink.

On the one hand, the UK and the US political systems are very different, but in reality, they aren't. Money and influence help in both. We need to the get money out of politics. Time to get the politicians out of the back pockets of the corporates and financiers. To begin with, we need to find a fair way to stop politicians leaving politics and going into high paying jobs where they peddle their influence, and we need to stop campaign contributions from companies and lobby groups.

Perhaps we can partially remove political parties from the debate and instead vote for representatives based on their individual merits. The voting form doesn't have to say which party they belong to, just what they stand for. To make that easy, perhaps we could have a few headings that they can give their viewpoints on: Income, Healthcare, Social Care, Education and the Environment; each candidate could put together a form with their stance on each topic.

It is time for politicians to represent the people and the people to know what they stand for.

Property

It's an asset that needs addressing separately and quickly. You can drive through many major cities like London, Toronto and New York and see apartment buildings with almost no lights on. No one lives there. The properties were bought by the world's wealthy including the Chinese, Russians, Arabs and the financiers, of course. Time to tax the hell out of properties that are not lived in by residents. Say 15% of the value of the property every year. Let's kill that market. It doesn't serve any useful purpose to the country. In fact, it does the exact opposite. It makes it too expensive for people to live and start businesses. Let's stop pandering to the super-rich. Most of these 'investors' bring little or no value to the local society. Tax them and some of them will hit the market and prices will drop.

And then we have the growing, and over-priced, property rental market. It would seem that localised rent control is the best way to deal with this. The council/local government of each area can fix the rent at 25% of the average salary, with tiers for differently sized properties. This would lower rents and stop PEG groups and other bad landlords. It would also help bring property prices back down. And if the property market crashes, why not use some trickle-up? The government can print money and buy properties for local councils who can then rent and/or sell them to local people.

This includes retail locations on the High Street (main street). Local government should own some of the High Street and rent it out so prices can be more realistic than they are now. A new business has great difficulty affording High Street rents these days.

Step Two – Social Valyou

People

We are social animals and we need a healthy environment. We are being rewarded for our basic economic value with UI and now we should be rewarded for our further contribution to society with a job and a paycheck. What are these jobs? What will replace all the jobs lost to the end of the automobile revolution? Where should we direct our energies? What will be our purpose?

Our new purpose should be 'social valyou'.

If people and the environment are the most important things to us, the things we value most, then surely our new purpose should be focused on them – on compassion for people and our environment and on activities that generate social value – not simply production. You can already see that is where the under thirty-fives are gravitating to. It's the one thing that AI and automation can never replace: compassion. Compassion is a basic human instinct. As our lives have gotten better our compassion has grown wider and deeper. Compassion unites us and encompasses people all over the world, regardless of tribe. Let's find and create compassionate jobs.

Let's develop more green and socially orientated projects and activities that are desperately needed in areas such as health, education, welfare, social services, the environment, and infrastructure. Why not throw people at them? They all need people!

As humans, we need to interact with other humans and the environment. It's in our DNA. Those that do so already live longer and have more fulfilling lives. And guess what, most of the scary issues we face today are around people and the environment. Wouldn't it be nice if we could solve two problems with one solution? Well, we can.

What does that mean in practical terms?

The NHS reports that in the UK there are more than two million people over seventy-five and living alone – and one million of them go more than a month without speaking to a neighbour, friend or family member and can go a week without interacting with anyone.[184] Age UK says that 6% of over sixty-fives leave their homes less than once a week.[185] This is criminal. Imagine how demoralising it is for that person. Close your eyes and just picture yourself going for a week without talking to anyone. No one. Not a soul. No one knows you exist. No one cares. The world has forgotten you and your contribution. You feel valueless. Shame on us!

These people are alone, yet we are social animals. They are in a mental prison and it's time to break them out. And we have the people to do it – young and old.

And no, I'm sorry, AI is not the answer. While it certainly has a role, and already does provide one, people still need people and companionship. And there are young people who need older people and what they can provide. Instead of paying a company to provide a live-in carer at £900 a week, plus food, lodging, utilities etc, which few elderly can afford, why not have a young, part-time carer live there for room and board and £100 a week? What about day-care? Same thing.

For those who watched the CH4 documentary on four-year-olds and pensioners you'll know what I am talking about. In only six weeks the results were amazing. Both groups benefitted tremendously, physically and mentally, and I have yet to meet someone who didn't shed a tear as one pensioner ran the egg and spoon race where only six-weeks earlier, she could barely walk with a Zimmer frame. It meant day-care and interaction, purpose and value – for both.

In other words, we can add value and feel of value by helping others, by doing things that benefit our fellow human beings. That is part of our value, as well as economic value.

Measuring and rewarding value is complicated. How do we account for things that we do, that do not generate 'money', but *do* enhance our own and others' lives? Raising children and charity work are two prime examples, both of which could be either 'free' or for cash. In a nutshell, how do we value 'free'? We're still contributing if we help a friend paint their new flat, but we're not being paid in cash – well maybe partially in pizza and beer – it's not for free, though we're giving ourselves, our time. It costs our valuable time. But it's a bitch to quantify.

144

Even free time has value. It's when we recharge our batteries, recharge our minds, rebuild our bodies and come up with the next great idea. An employee who gets no breaks simply doesn't work as productively. A professional athlete can't play all day, every day. Not only would their performance plummet, but they wouldn't be able to do it. Both our minds and bodies need to recharge, otherwise they crash and burn.

It's the same for those trees and plants growing in your fields. They're of value to the bees, bugs and other wildlife – and in turn, to us. But, we don't put 'value' on them until they are used to 'produce' something like a chair, honey or a loaf of bread. We need the natural environment but mostly only seem to ascribe value to it when we knock it down.

We need to focus on the value we give and take. How much we produce is no longer humankind's goal, its prime directive. It's now more about social value. We should be rewarded for the contribution of our time. We humans, and the time we contribute to the greater society, should be our currency.

Social valyou as the new currency

Valuing people in this instance is fairly straightforward and roughly in place already.

People's time is quantified, and we are rewarded for its use. It's how we add value, how we spend our precious time. Most people's time is already valued and paid for in the proverbial paycheck. Even if the 'bang for buck' of the rewarding of time is not in balance. The Hedge Funds and PEGs people are simply not as socially valuable as thousands of teachers and nurses. Each $1bn they take through financial engineering would pay for 20,000 people on $50,000 a year. What's more valuable, one bean counter or 20,000 teachers? I think most people would have to agree, that's a no-brainer.

Time is already pretty much the currency of 95% of the world, embodied in our paychecks. Whether you are paid by the hour or have a fixed salary, you are being paid for your time. Whether you're a delivery driver, gardener, doctor, teacher or rocket scientist, you're essentially being paid by the hour. Your time is already measured and has a value attached.

The more productive we are with our time or the more specialised a knowledge required for the use of our time, the more we are usually paid. But, many salaries may not be correct in relation to their social value. With UI and proper taxation however, this should balance itself out fairly quickly.

People's time is what's valuable. If we measured people's time and based GDP on it, things would be a lot clearer. With UI, we'd all have a minimum base value: the value we add, by simply being here and helping the economy by purchasing other people's goods and services. We are all worth something to society and the economy. Add that to our paychecks and you have the value of the entire country, the total of each person's total value (UI + job).

As it is now, GDP is not as informative as it could be. It is based on the old theory that we should always produce more, and there are some glaring problems with how we compute it. It's not fit for purpose any longer as it's trying to measure our outdated goal of producing more.

Take a couple with children. If they hire a babysitter for their children, that's accounted for in GDP because they pay them with money. If one person stays at home and takes care of the child, it's not counted as part of GDP as it's unpaid. In both cases, someone spent their valuable time doing a valuable activity. But currently we only put GDP value on the one where money changes hands, even though they are exactly the same activity.

Charity work is the same. If you are paid by the charity it's part of GDP, if you spend twenty hours a week working for a charity for no money, it's not. Again, in both cases you are applying your valuable time and helping the charity add value, but only one person is accounted for in the stats. Both people's time is just as valuable and contributes just as much to the charity. Yet, they're not recognised equally.

Sure, this is an oversimplification, but you can see where I'm headed. Now what do we do?

There are two things necessary to create anything: people and the environment. These are what are important, and although they may appear seemingly 'free' at times, they aren't. There are only so many trees and we only have so much time. Together we are the analogue world and we create value by taking from our time and/or the environment. We've established our *valyou* based on time, now it's time to factor in the environment. It needs pricing, aka *valyouing*.

The Environment – The Natural World We Inhabit

Carbon credit is a start, but far more is needed. Climate change is an international emergency. We need to establish values based on the physical environment. As an example, if you chop down a tree to make a chair but plant another one to replace it, then your eco balance is flat. If you plant two trees, you add positive value, you get an eco-credit. If you take oil out of the ground and use it for power, you create negative value, you get an eco-debit. You can't replace it after all. If you use solar panels to generate power, you're eco flat or positive, so there will be an impetus to use less oil and more renewable power and clean energy.

In *social valyou* terms, the new way to measure GDP would be based on the use of our time combined with environmental costs. Once we have this in place, we can then measure our true environmental costs and include them in GDP.

GDP, as it's currently measured, is very complex, with a variety of different items being added and removed from its computations. And it includes different things in different countries. In other words, it isn't accurate or actually recording what is important to us. If we measure the value of people's time and environmental value however, this changes. GDP would become a true measure of the value we are creating and far easier to measure. Instead of trying to measure the value of all the shoes or computers sold, it would measure the value of everyone involved in making the shoes or computers, and what they received in compensation, our pay packets, plus the cost to the environment.

Let's refer to this new form of GDP (Gross Domestic Product) as **GDV** (Gross Domestic Value) and also define some other new terms:

- **GPV** – Gross People Value. UI plus all the salaries of everyone. That was easy. We could measure that tomorrow. And whether you're taking care of a child, helping out at a charity or helping a friend to paint a room, this value will now be accounted for in GPV.
- **GEV** – Gross Environment Value. This could be a plus or a minus and would measure the environmental costs the country has

incurred, for both production and disposal. We want this to be flat or even positive.
- **GBV** – Gross Business Value. The total income of all businesses, minus or plus their Environment Value.

The gift that just keeps giving. GDV can be the basis of a currency. The new social valyou currency would be based around people's time and the environment. Recording a global currency is easy – it's digital, it's blockchain – and there can even be physical printing (cash). Gotta keep the black market happy.

The three GDV measures can be tallied, compared and measured globally. Everyone can keep their currencies while at the same time fixing international exchange rates. The US can keep its $ and the UK can keep its £, but they can only print more of them based on the increase in GDV. Yeah, the governments won't like that – and if they print more, the currencies will depreciate. As everyone would know the value behind the currency, the GDV, the transparent market will set the correct exchange rate based on the GDV.

'Hold on a minute!' I hear you say. 'We're a globalised world. How can GDV be enforced when the environmental costs are global?' Good question, but there are no problems, only solutions. We cannot expect a developing country not to exploit its environment. After all, we did it. But, we can reward them for exploiting the environment properly and being socially responsible. Many countries and political/economic blocs have environmental protection agencies already, including the US, the UK and the EU, and they work with others around the globe. They just need an international scoring system that can be tallied in the price of products.

Let's take a factory in China or India. It may be cheaper for them to access coal-fired electricity today, which is bad for the environment. But, solar, wind, waves or other renewable energies may still be expensive and would push up their production costs. They don't want to do this. But, that's today.

To persuade them it's worth their while to take part, we can attach a GEV score to each product; a negative score for coal added to each product and a flat or positive score to each product using renewables. And then yes, the end consumer, us, will have to pick up the tab because we will have to pay more. But, capitalism can kick into gear here. In order to keep costs down, companies here will push the manufacturers there, companies like Apple and Nike, to switch to renewables, in order to lower the sales price.

But that won't be enough. We need a Green Revolution.

We live in a disposable society. Things have too short a shelf life. It's killing the environment. This has to change. If the costs go up for that iPhone, due to environmental charges in manufacturing and disposal, then people will want it to last longer. Apple and the other phone manufactures would then be motivated to start building modular phones and stop selling phones with built-in obsolescence. They'll make renewable products. It will be in their self-interest – pure capitalism at work.

Having *social valyou* as the basis of a new global currency is self-checking and will stop further discrepancies happening. In order to earn more and to pay you more, companies and the government will need to be more productive with both people and the environment. It will be in everyone's interest to keep environmental debits down or even positive.

Conclusion

We still have old-school problems to solve, no doubt, but we also have some new issues. Issues we're having trouble getting our heads around. Attention spans are dropping, and anxiety is increasing, particularly among the young. Surely it should be the other way around? After all, food, shelter and clothing are basically taken care of, especially for them. We're safe and we have free time. Why on earth aren't we happy instead of anxious?

Previously we worked. Our work produced value (money) and made us feel valuable (esteem). Thing is, we don't need to over-produce anymore. In fact, our production usefulness is rapidly diminishing, and people are simply not needed in a lot of production today. So, what is our purpose, if not to produce more and better? What is our value? This is a Level 4 problem. It's a 'first world problem', but far from trivial.

We seem to have reached a turning point. We don't know what the future holds, but we know it will be very different to where we are now. We need to decide how we want to grow up. What is our purpose? How do we add value? Why do we get up in the morning? Suicides are mostly a Level 4 issue, as is anxiety, and are at their highest since the second world war in the US.[186] Why?

Lack of purpose and value seem to be part of what's causing this stress and anxiety.[187] And yes, to reiterate, I know this is a generalisation; an oversimplification necessary to keep us focused on the forest and not the trees. But, the problem will grow if we don't address it.

How civil a society do we want? I mean this in both senses of the word 'civil' as it relates to ordinary citizens and government, as well as meaning polite and courteous. What do we want our society to look like? Logically, it seems that we need to take our strengths from the past and focus them for our future. We need to understand the good and the bad: how to deal with finance, globalisation, politics and AI (Artificial Intelligence), which are critical for our future – and, of course, the environment.

It's all about value. What do we put value on? What do we think is valuable? The answer of course is people and the environment. We are currently living in a world where there appears to be a conspiracy against humanity led by financiers and politicians. Half the people over forty feel this way, as do most of the people under forty. Time to push back. Time to evolve.

All of us alive at this very moment, whether born today or a hundred years ago, find ourselves at a major point in the evolution of humankind. We have some big problems to sort out, but we also have some amazing opportunities. And we all have something to contribute. We have *valyou*.

There is a lot in flux in society. Some people feel all is relatively fine and they want everything to stay as is. But, it's impossible. Civilisation/society is always changing, and particularly quickly at the moment. Some people want minor changes. A growing number of people want big changes. We can feel it, taste it. We know something is afoot. It's in the air. Things have changed, but we're not quite sure how or what. With 200,000 years of built-in reflexes, it takes time to change – to adapt. Especially if we don't know what needs changing and what we're adapting to. The big picture is changing.

And we're not addressing this directly. We're trying to manage the individual pieces using yesterday's thinking and tools. But it's the big picture that has changed. Humankind's purpose is simply not what it used to be. What we value is changing – from production value to *social valyou*.

How best do we protect future generations and send them on their way? What values do we have that we would like to pass on to them? Which ones would best serve them and humankind? Which values are in the midst of change already? The tipping point of humankind's evolution was the removal of the worry about survival. The need to produce has to be replaced. We need a new purpose – a new reason to get up in the morning. We need something else to motivate us, as almost all of us want to add value. It's deep in our nature, as are compassion and competition.

The answer is to *valyou* humankind and the environment much more. And our purpose is to proactively add value to them, not just to produce things and make money. Our value is as custodians of the planet – humanity and the environment.

Now that we have taken care of many of our physical needs, it's time to focus on our emotional needs. Our ultimate goal must be for people to be able to feel of value by doing something that is socially valuable. We need to 'make a difference'. Part of the solution is in the problem itself. Interaction with others, and indeed feeling valued, is what study after study shows is the best thing for our physical health and mental wellbeing. Nothing tops people.

We've identified the issues, now what do we do about addressing them?

For a start, we need to think about people in the future differently. Our grandchildren won't be like us, even less than we are like our grandparents of a hundred years ago. Their 'basic needs' may be similar to today, but how we provide those things will be very different.

One of the wonderful things about people is that we are competitive, with ourselves, with others and with our environment. We strive to do better and to be better. It's how we went from hunter- gatherers to where we are. Now, we need to focus our attention and let our naturally competitive spirit out.

Our current systems around the world have their good points and their bad points, but regardless, they are yesterday's systems and they're not fit for purpose. They were not designed for what we're facing, and they are being exploited by the rich and powerful. They were designed to provide more stuff. Yesterday's systems were not created to deal with AI or the humanity-threatening environmental issues that face us, nor the financial inequality that surrounds us.

We need to retool our political and economic systems for tomorrow. We need to correct the glaring financial inequality that exits today. We've seen how this is something that can be achieved fairly easily using social taxes. We also need to ensure that there is not mass deprivation and that consumer spending, the bulk of the economy, continues.

As we've also seen, Universal Income is the obvious answer. Not only will UI remove social deprivation and attain more equality, but it will also encourage entrepreneurship, the arts and volunteer work.

We need to deal with the end of the automobile revolution and the associated unemployment it will create, as well as the lack of resources for social services. We can accomplish this by creating more social roles. When I say social roles, I mean this in a very broad sense, green and people centred, ranging from teaching archery or fort building to kids (or adults), to helping older people get around or keeping them company, to planting trees and taking care of the environment and starting green businesses, and so on. Doing things that are of value to us. We can create a Green Revolution. We can create a People Revolution. We can evolve.

We also need to deal with ML and AI because their impact on humanity is not trifling. This is some serious sh*t. While we have to be careful, their future growth and impacts are inevitable, so we might as well get with the program. Progress cannot be stopped. But it can be directed. While we may not know if AI will ever achieve consciousness, it would be prudent to assume that it will. That being the case, we need to figure out how best to protect ourselves. If AI becomes conscious, it must consciously not want to harm us, or the environment. If AI gains consciousness, it will be due partly to nature and partly to nurture, as with children. And we can't predict the outcome. But we can influence it, not by having a 'prime directive', but by clearly deciding what values we want to pass onto it, to teach it. And then hope for the best.

It's crucial we get this right. Our decisions will dictate whether we have a future that resembles Star Trek, one where there's good social order and 'fairness' or one that resembles Blade Runner and its dystopia. The future is an exciting opportunity that we should all embrace. Together, we can solve the problems we face today, as well as move humanity to its next level. We need to evolve.

It's time for change. We need to *valyou* humanity and the environment – not just production and money. *Social Valyou* needs to be the new currency.

Acknowledgments

I would never have pulled this off without Julie, you're a superstar. I held my breathe on the first read wondering if you'd 'get it'. You did! Tig persevered through multiple revisions, Margaret sorted my bad language and Hussein kept pushing me, thank you.

And heartfelt thanks to my wonderful family and friends who've put up with me and my musings.

[1] Factfulness: Ten reasons we're wrong about the world, Hans Rosling, Ola Rosling, Anna Rosling Ronnlund

[2] https://www.fircroft.com/blogs/the-automotive-industry-employs-more-people-than-you-think-71462610395

[3] https://www.fircroft.com/blogs/the-automotive-industry-employs-more-people-than-you-think-71462610395

[4] https://www.acea.be/automobile-industry/facts-about-the-industry

[5] https://www.marketwatch.com/story/keep-on-truckin-in-a-majority-of-states-its-the-most-popular-job-2015-02-09

[6] http://www.alltrucking.com/faq/truck-drivers-in-the-usa/

[7] https://www.makeuseof.com/tag/self-driving-cars-endanger-millions-american-jobs-thats-okay/

[8] https://www.theguardian.com/technology/2016/apr/07/convoy-self-driving-trucks-completes-first-european-cross-border-trip

[9] https://www.digitaltrends.com/cars/why-are-people-in-japan-renting-cars-but-not-driving-them-anywhere/

[10] https://www.topviewnyc.com/packages/how-much-25-major-cities-make-in-parking-ticket-revenue-per-capita

[11] https://www.bbc.com/news/uk-england-london-50445636

[12] https://www.petrolprices.com/news/councils-made-record-profit-year-parking-fines/

[13] https://fortune.com/2016/03/13/cars-parked-95-percent-of-time/

[14] https://www.gapminder.org/topics/four-income-levels/

[15] Factfulness: Ten reasons we're wrong about the world, Hans Rosling, Ola Rosling, Anna Rosling Ronnlund

[16] https://edition.cnn.com/2018/12/05/asia/japan-vacant-akiya-ghost-homes/index.html?no-st=1561902521

[17] https://www.irishtimes.com/news/science/earth-s-population-may-start-to-fall-from-2040-does-it-matter-1.3808527?mode=amp

[18] https://www.cbc.ca/radio/day6/episode-428-bissonnette-s-sentence-art-forgery-k-pop-at-the-grammys-leolist-human-trafficking-and-more-1.5009885/empty-planet-is-the-threat-of-overpopulation-a-myth-1.5009923

[19] https://www.worldometers.info/world-population/

[20] Empty Planet: Darrel Bricker and John Ibbitson.

[21] https://www.irishtimes.com/news/science/earth-s-population-may-start-to-fall-from-2040-does-it-matter-1.3808527?mode=amp

[22] https://www.businessinsider.com/italian-villages-selling-dollar-homes-2019-2?r=US&IR=T

[23] https://www.theguardian.com/world/2019/sep/11/underpopulated-italian-region-molise

[24] https://www.businessinsider.com/japan-giving-away-abandoned-homes-free-2018-12?r=US&IR=T

[25] https://www.rcn.org.uk/news-and-events/news/removing-the-student-nurse-bursary-has-been-a-disaster

[26] https://www.independent.co.uk/news/health/nurses-drop-out-graduation-royal-college-bursaries-a8519926.html

[27] https://www.theguardian.com/society/2017/jun/12/96-drop-in-eu-nurses-registering-to-work-in-britain-since-brexit-vote

[28] http://www.nationalhealthexecutive.com/Health-Care-News/nhs-nursing-shortages-risk-becoming-a-national-emergency

[29] https://markets.businessinsider.com/news/stocks/aging-demographics-impact-on-economy-growth-markets-2019-2-1027968236

[30] https://www.independent.co.uk/news/uk/politics/eu-workers-uk-tax-treasury-brexit-migrants-british-citizens-a8542506.html

[31] https://www.ons.gov.uk/economy/governmentpublicsectorandtaxes/publicsectorfinance/articles/theukcontributiontotheeubudget/2017-10-31

[32] https://www.msn.com/en-gb/news/brexit/brexit-will-soon-have-cost-the-uk-more-than-all-of-its-payments-to-the-eu-over-the-last-47-years-put-together/ar-BBYWF39?ocid=sw

[33] https://www.pbs.org/newshour/economy/making-sense/4-myths-about-how-immigrants-affect-the-u-s-economy

[34] https://immigrationforum.org/article/immigrants-as-economic-contributors-immigrant-tax-contributions-and-spending-power/

[35] https://www.independent.co.uk/life-style/gadgets-and-tech/news/facebook-artificial-intelligence-ai-own-language-what-does-it-mean-fair-robots-chatbots-a7874576.html

[36] https://www.technologyreview.com/lists/innovators-under-35/2019/visionary/azalia-mirhoseini/

[37] https://en.wikipedia.org/wiki/Trolley_problem

[38] https://www.technologyreview.com/s/612341/a-global-ethics-study-aims-to-help-ai-solve-the-self-driving-trolley-problem/?utm_source=facebook.com&utm_medium=social&utm_campaign=owned_social

[39] https://www.imdb.com/title/tt4122068/?ref_=ttvi_tt

[40] https://aerospace.org/article/danger-orbital-debris
[41] https://edition.cnn.com/2019/03/13/tech/oneweb-space-debris-junk-low-earth-orbit/
[42] https://edition.cnn.com/2019/03/13/tech/oneweb-space-debris-junk-low-earth-orbit/
[43] https://time.com/5652972/july-2019-hottest-month/?utm_source=newsletter&utm_medium=email&utm_campaign=the-brief-pm&utm_content=20190815&xid=newsletter-brief
[44] https://time.com/5610084/canadas-permafrost-thawing-surprising/
[45] https://www.theguardian.com/world/2019/jul/31/putin-sends-military-fight-siberia-forest-fires-russia
[46] https://edition.cnn.com/2020/01/01/australia/australia-fires-explainer-intl-hnk-scli/index.html
[47] https://www.youtube.com/watch?v=TQmz6Rbpnu0
[48] https://www.ipcc.ch/site/assets/uploads/2018/11/AR6_brochure_en.pdf
[49] https://www.opendemocracy.net/en/opendemocracyuk/these-figures-show-how-out-of-touch-uk-politicians-are-from-everyone-else/
[50] https://qz.com/1190595/the-typical-us-congress-member-is-12-times-richer-than-the-typical-american-household/
[51] https://edition.cnn.com/2018/03/05/politics/donald-trump-xi-jinping-analysis/index.html
[52] https://www.theguardian.com/politics/2019/aug/14/johnson-sparks-cross-party-backlash-over-brexit-collaboration-claim
[53] https://edition.cnn.com/2017/08/15/politics/trump-charlottesville-delay/index.html
[54] https://edition.cnn.com/2019/08/23/us/trump-obama-change-blake/index.html?no-st=1566570795
[55] https://www.bloomberg.com/graphics/2016-brexit-referendum/
[56] https://www.independent.co.uk/news/uk/politics/brexit-leave-eu-remain-vote-support-against-poll-uk-europe-final-say-yougov-second-referendum-peter-a8541971.html
[57] https://en.wikipedia.org/wiki/2016_United_States_presidential_election
[58] https://www.theguardian.com/politics/ng-interactive/2019/dec/12/uk-general-election-2019-full-results-live-labour-conservatives-tories
[59] https://www.theguardian.com/environment/2020/jan/25/climate-change-election-2020-youth-activism

[60] https://www.edinburghnews.scotsman.com/news/pupils-outraged-edinburgh-council-ban-them-climate-protests-542763
[61] https://www.forbes.com/sites/noahkirsch/2017/11/09/the-3-richest-americans-hold-more-wealth-than-bottom-50-of-country-study-finds/#723240a3cf86
[62] https://edition.cnn.com/2019/01/20/business/oxfam-billionaires-davos/index.html?utm_term=link&utm_source=fbCNN&utm_content=2019-01-21T02%3A31%3A11&utm_medium=social
[63] https://thehill.com/policy/finance/476103-worlds-richest-500-people-saw-their-wealth-jump-25-percent-in-2019
[64] https://www.peoplespolicyproject.org/2019/06/14/top-1-up-21-trillion-bottom-50-down-900-billion/
[65] https://www.taxjustice.net/topics/inequality-democracy/inequality-tax-havens/
[66] https://en.wikipedia.org/wiki/Wealth_inequality_in_the_United_States
[67] https://en.wikipedia.org/wiki/Wealth_inequality_in_the_United_States
[68] https://patrioticmillionaires.org/
[69] https://www.ted.com/talks/nick_hanauer_beware_fellow_plutocrats_the_pitchforks_are_coming
[70] https://www.businessinsider.com/warren-buffett-on-the-ovarian-lottery-2013-12
[71] https://money.cnn.com/2013/03/04/news/economy/buffett-secretary-taxes/index.html
[72] https://www.technologyreview.com/s/610395/if-youre-so-smart-why-arent-you-rich-turns-out-its-just-chance/
[73] https://en.wikipedia.org/wiki/Fiat_money
[74] https://www.investopedia.com/terms/f/fiatmoney.asp
[75] https://www.technologyreview.com/f/613201/nearly-all-bitcoin-trades-are-fake-apparently/
[76] https://medium.com/futuresin/my-favorite-facebook-conspiracy-might-be-true-bf153c217773
[77] https://www.youtube.com/watch?v=qMXseN8d_lY&feature=youtu.be
[78] https://www.bbc.com/news/technology-49343262
[79] https://edition.cnn.com/2019/04/11/tech/amazon-alexa-listening/index.html

[80] https://www.theverge.com/2019/7/12/20692524/facebook-five-billion-ftc-fine-embarrassing-joke

[81] https://onezero.medium.com/prison-time-is-the-answer-to-techs-privacy-crisis-53da1559124f

[82] https://en.wikipedia.org/wiki/Bancor

[83] https://www.marketwatch.com/story/how-bernie-sanders-and-alexandria-ocasio-cortezs-proposal-to-cap-credit-card-interest-rates-at-15-could-hurt-consumers-2019-05-10

[84] Makers and Takers: Rana Foroohar

[85] Makers and Takers: Rana Foroohar chapter 6

[86] https://www.institutionalinvestor.com/article/b1dtk9138hd0d9/When-Buyout-Firms-Step-in-Watch-Out

[87] https://www.businessinsider.com/private-equity-firms-making-fortune-stripping-capital-out-of-companies-2017-10?r=US&IR=T

[88] https://www.businessinsider.com/private-equity-firms-making-fortune-stripping-capital-out-of-companies-2017-10?r=US&IR=T

[89] https://www.theguardian.com/business/2007/feb/23/privateequity1

[90] https://www.theguardian.com/business/2017/feb/28/philip-green-agrees-pay-363m-bhs-pension-fund

[91] https://www.theguardian.com/business/2017/feb/28/philip-green-agrees-pay-363m-bhs-pension-fund

[92] https://www.itv.com/news/2016-07-25/thousands-of-bhs-staff-to-be-told-of-redundancies/

[93] https://www.theatlantic.com/magazine/archive/2018/07/toys-r-us-bankruptcy-private-equity/561758/

[94] https://www.theguardian.com/business/2004/jul/01/utilities

[95] https://www.ft.com/content/66ff64e4-fa9d-11e3-8959-00144feab7de

[96] https://www.theguardian.com/business/2012/dec/17/comet-closes-remaining-shops

[97] https://www.bisnow.com/london/news/multifamily/private-equity-is-finding-ways-to-help-solve-the-uks-housing-crisis-and-make-a-profit-too-83653

[98] https://www.ft.com/content/d667c6e4-605c-11e9-9300-0becfc937c37

[99] https://www.thetimes.co.uk/article/same-old-story-when-private-equity-owners-sell-out-v9bj87dct

[100] https://www.vox.com/2016/5/10/11648746/hedge-fund-manager-

earnings

[101] https://www.bravenewfilms.org/billionairesvsteachers

[102] Makers and Takers: Rana Foroohar

[103] https://www.independent.co.uk/news/world/politics/rich-have-only-got-richer-since-2000-davos-a6823281.html

[104] https://www.bloomberg.com/news/articles/2019-01-04/u-k-ceo-pay-to-top-average-worker-s-2019-income-by-lunchtime

[105] https://www.theguardian.com/technology/2017/oct/10/american-trucker-automation-jobs

[106] https://prospect.org/article/neoliberalism-political-success-economic-failure

[107] https://www.theguardian.com/books/2016/apr/15/neoliberalism-ideology-problem-george-monbiot

[108] https://www.theguardian.com/commentisfree/2019/jun/12/why-are-we-still-pretending-trickle-down-economics-work

[109] https://www.businessinsider.com/us-budget-deficit-hits-record-february-national-debt-2019-3

[110] Makers and Takers: Rana Foroohar

[111] https://www.cbsnews.com/news/japans-palace-grounds-once-more-valuable-than-california/

[112] https://www.thebalance.com/apple-stock-vs-apple-bonds-which-is-the-better-buy-417113

[113] Makers and Takers: Rana Foroohar

[114] https://www.imdb.com/title/tt1596363/

[115] https://insight.kellogg.northwestern.edu/article/what-went-wrong-at-aig

[116] https://www.investopedia.com/articles/economics/09/american-investment-group-aig-bailout.asp

[117] https://www.housingwire.com/articles/48786-ge-to-pay-15-billion-fine-over-wmc-mortgage-subprime-loans

[118] http://money.com/money/4709270/americans-die-in-debt/

[119] https://www.msn.com/en-us/money/personalfinance/on-average-americans-die-with-dollar61000-in-debt-who-pays/ar-BBMBgqM

[120] http://nymag.com/intelligencer/2011/03/citibank_received_more_bailout.html

[121] https://www.ft.com/content/1e63b3b0-d7e1-11e1-80a8-00144feabdc0

[122] http://www.in2013dollars.com/1914-dollars-in-2018?amount=5
[123] https://en.wikipedia.org/wiki/Nick_Hanauer
[124] https://www.theguardian.com/money/2016/nov/02/institute-for-economic-affairs-report-abolish-20-taxes-income-tax-15-per-cent
[125] https://www.bbc.co.uk/news/uk-politics-22575135
[126] https://www.cheatsheet.com/entertainment/the-real-reason-bill-gates-children-wont-inherit-much-of-his-fortune.html/
[127] https://www.cnbc.com/2015/03/09/boomers-mimic-warren-buffett-when-it-comes-to-inheritances.html
[128] https://www.independent.co.uk/news/business/news/finance-curse-uk-economy-sector-city-of-london-loss-financial-services-a8571036.html
[129] https://www.businessinsider.com/amazon-size-insane-facts-about-company-2017-9?r=US&IR=T
[130] https://media.thinknum.com/articles/how-big-is-amazon-a-look-at-the-mind-bending-numbers/
[131] https://qz.com/1196256/it-took-amazon-amzn-14-years-to-make-as-much-net-profit-as-it-did-in-the-fourth-quarter-of-2017/
[132] https://www.macrotrends.net/stocks/charts/AMZN/amazon/revenue
[133] https://www.ft.com/content/4d85c99c-bb44-11e8-8274-55b72926558f
[134] Makers and Takers: Rana Foroohar
[135] https://www.thebalance.com/consumer-debt-statistics-causes-and-impact-3305704
[136] https://www.cnbc.com/2018/02/13/total-us-household-debt-soars-to-record-above-13-trillion.html
[137] https://www.forbes.com/sites/zackfriedman/2019/05/08/student-loans-betsy-devos-sale/
[138] https://medium.com/@letterforawealthtax/an-open-letter-to-the-2020-presidential-candidates-its-time-to-tax-us-more-6eb3a548b2fe
[139] https://www.vox.com/future-perfect/2019/6/25/18744218/billionaires-2020-candidates-wealth-tax-open-letter-elizabeth-warren
[140] https://www.reddit.com/r/BasicIncome/wiki/index#wiki_that.27s_all_very_well.2C_but_where.27s_the_evidence.3F
[141] https://www.vox.com/policy-and-politics/2018/2/13/16997188/alaska-basic-income-permanent-fund-oil-

revenue-study

[142] https://time.com/5571472/basic-income-society-problems/

[143] https://www.theguardian.com/cities/2018/jun/27/benefit-or-burden-the-cities-trying-out-universal-basic-income

[144] https://www.inverse.com/article/53466-basic-income-canada-s-trial-had-a-huge-effect-on-people-s-health

[145] https://www.technologyreview.com/s/611418/basic-income-could-work-if-you-do-it-canada-style/

[146] https://www.ukpublicspending.co.uk/year_spending_2018UKbn_17bc1n_40#ukgs302

[147] https://www.ukpublicspending.co.uk/year_spending_2018UKbn_17bc1n_404400#ukgs302

[148] https://www.chroniclelive.co.uk/news/north-east-news/hmp-frankland-most-notorious-prisoners-15332522

[149] https://cpag.org.uk/child-poverty/child-poverty-facts-and-figures

[150] https://people.com/human-interest/ryan-kyote-school-lunch-debt-allowance-california/

[151] https://abcnews.go.com/US/rhode-island-school-district-serve-students-owe-lunch/story?id=62905116

[152] https://www.independent.co.uk/news/health/nhs-latest-senior-doctors-hospitals-underfunding-accelerate-privatisation-agenda-conservative-a7808591.html

[153] https://www.independent.co.uk/news/uk/politics/student-loan-debt-interest-rates-government-a9054806.html

[154] https://www.cnbc.com/2019/05/19/billionaire-tells-morehouse-seniors-hell-pay-off-their-student-loans.html

[155] https://edition.cnn.com/2019/08/15/business/china-solar-electricity-scli-intl/index.html?utm_source=fbCNN&utm_medium=social&utm_content=2019-08-15T16%3A00%3A44&utm_term=link

[156] https://www.bbc.com/news/world-asia-china-51171491

[157] https://edition.cnn.com/2019/08/08/world/ipcc-report-land-climate-crisis-sci-intl/

[158] https://www.goodnewsnetwork.org/eu-approves-groundbreaking-right-to-repair-laws/

[159] https://www.mercurynews.com/2019/08/20/new-report-california-has-five-times-more-clean-energy-jobs-than-fossil-fuel-jobs/

[160] https://www.theguardian.com/environment/2019/aug/01/fossil-fuel-subsidy-cash-pay-green-energy-transition

[161] https://www.techradar.com/news/dummy-40-ways-graphene-is-about-to-change-your-life

[162] https://www.technologyreview.com/s/613267/borophene-the-new-2d-material-taking-chemistry-by-storm/

[163] https://time.com/5609508/social-support-health-benefits/?utm_source=time.com&utm_medium=email&utm_campaign=the-brief&utm_content=2019070811am&xid=newsletter-brief

[164] https://www.hrsa.gov/enews/past-issues/2019/january-17/loneliness-epidemic

[165] https://medium.com/swlh/the-tesla-bombshell-almost-nobody-is-talking-about-robotaxis-930556d9f965?source=email-32e3dd0890fc-1563686983434-digest.reader------1-50------------------2e43c726_5969_45bb_80e9_bc65ca413f52-12

[166] https://medium.com/@marcsabatierhvidkjr/how-does-a-danish-mcdonalds-worker-make-20-hour-without-a-minimum-wage-law-ea8bcbaa870f

[167] https://medium.com/@marcsabatierhvidkjr/how-does-a-danish-mcdonalds-worker-make-20-hour-without-a-minimum-wage-law-ea8bcbaa870f

[168] https://medium.com/fast-company/gmail-keeps-a-record-of-your-purchase-history-in-plain-sight-and-its-not-alone-5d0089aeceb5

[169] https://www.zdnet.com/article/in-2018-aws-delivered-most-of-amazons-operating-income/

[170] https://en.wikipedia.org/wiki/Amazon_Web_Services

[171] https://www.telegraph.co.uk/news/uknews/1533054/Britain-the-most-spied-on-nation-in-the-world.html

[172] https://www.independent.co.uk/news/world/asia/china-police-facial-recognition-technology-ai-jaywalkers-fines-text-wechat-weibo-cctv-a8279531.html

[173] https://venturebeat.com/2019/10/11/ai-weekly-in-china-you-can-no-longer-buy-a-smartphone-without-a-face-scan/

[174] https://www.cityam.com/eu-considers-giving-citizens-explicit-rights-over-facial-recognition-data/

[175] https://www.businessinsider.com/swedish-people-embed-microchips-under-skin-to-replace-id-cards-2018-5?r=US&IR=T

[176] https://en.wikipedia.org/wiki/Pretty_Good_Privacy

[177] https://www.eff.org/deeplinks/2019/10/open-letter-governments-

us-uk-and-australia-facebook-all-out-attack-encryption

[178] https://www.neowin.net/news/cyber-criminals-are-using-a-stolen-nsa-tool-to-carry-out-digital-attacks-in-baltimore/

[179] https://en.wikipedia.org/wiki/WannaCry_ransomware_attack

[180] https://www.independent.co.uk/news/uk/home-news/nhs-hack-wanna-decryptor-ransomware-what-is-it-how-does-it-work-computer-a7733141.html

[181] https://www.theregister.co.uk/2020/01/09/amazon_ring_workers_fired/

[182] https://www.telegraph.co.uk/news/2017/03/07/wikileaks-claims-mi5-cia-developed-spyware-turn-samsung-tvs/

[183] https://www.theverge.com/2017/4/25/15421326/smart-tv-hacking-cia-samsung-weeping-angel-vulnerability

[184] https://www.nhs.uk/conditions/stress-anxiety-depression/loneliness-in-older-people/

[185] https://www.ageuk.org.uk/globalassets/age-uk/documents/reports-and-publications/reports-and-briefings/health--wellbeing/rb_june15_lonelines_in_later_life_evidence_review.pdf

[186] https://time.com/5609124/us-suicide-rate-increase/

[187] https://time.com/5550803/depression-suicide-rates-youth/

Printed in Great Britain
by Amazon